THE EMPTY SEAT

The Mindset of Soul Winning

HARRY OLSEN

Hope Broker Publishing

The Empty Seat, The Mindset of Soul Winning

by Harry Olsen

Hope Broker Publishing

www.HopeBrokerPublishing.com

Aurora, Colorado, 80013

Print ISBN: 978-0-578-96746-2

Library of Congress Control Number: 2021916137

Photo 97915950 © Andriy Petrenko | Dreamstime.com

Photo 531159865 MediaProduction | iStockphoto.com

Interior formatting by Ben Wolf

www.benwolf.com/editing-services

First Printing: 2021

Printed in The United States of America

This book is dedicated to servants of God.

The first is my dad, Missionary Marlin Olsen. The mindset of soul winning that drives me is a direct result of having been raised as his son.

The next is my mom, Gladys, who was an excellent balance to my dad's level of ministry fervor by lovingly lifting each of us children to our individual possibilities in serving Christ.

And to Carol, my wife. As you will see in reading this book, she is a main character alongside of me in this journey. I enthusiastically place her side by side with my parents in this dedication of the record of my personal passion.

I also want to dedicate this book to our three children, Rebekah, Josh, and Tim, who were, as children and young people, on this ministry rollercoaster with me.

To all of you, thank you for your part in helping me be productive in life and ministry.

"God's not dead - He's truly alive! In *The Empty Seat,* Harry Olsen records what Jesus continues to do as the risen and exalted head of the church through the Holy Spirit. His stories ignite a passion for sharing hope with a hurting world. My passion is discipling women, so this book will become a part of our spiritual journeys.

I want the women to see the power of the Holy Spirit is alive and possible in their lives. As they step out and live for the Lord, a watching world will see Jesus. This is the book, the spark I have been waiting for. I will read and reread it with my sisters in Christ every year."

Deblyn Freemon, author of
Come and See - Stepping out to follow Christ, Reading Through the Gospels, and
Go! I am sending you! - Learning from the Early Church: Acts, James, Galatians and 1,2 Thessalonians

"I've known Harry since the beginning of the 1990s. As a church planter, he had a great influence on my own ministry when we planted TurningPoint many years ago because of his passion for souls. He believes that there is not a spiritual gift of evangelism but that it is the commission and responsibility of every believer to share the message of salvation through surrender to Jesus. Because this conviction runs deep, he is always about that business.

I highly recommend that you incorporate the teaching in this book in your personal life and the local church. Not only are the real-life examples worth the read, but they are inspiring as well!"

Rod Shockley
TurningPoint Community Church
Auburn, Washington

"This is a refreshing look at evangelism for every believer. Certainly not just a How-To book, but also a narrative approach. Pastor Olsen shares success stories from his life that result in lives being impacted and changed because he *expected* the Holy Spirit to prepare the soil befitting the circumstance.

He shows it is through our gifts, talents, and personal lives that the Lord reaches through us to touch and change lives. As the Academic Dean for a distance learning program for church leadership, I find this book to be a great resource for our students."

Louis Mann
Academic Dean Ministry EquipNet

"There are many good books on evangelism which explain how to do it. This book is different. What Harry Olsen does in *The Empty Seat* is to tell of the amazing opportunities God has given him to share the good news about Jesus. Harry teaches evangelism not by telling us what to do, but showing us how it is done, and giving us its theological basis.

The stories Harry Olsen relates in *The Empty Seat* are embedded with biblical principles which readers can glean and apply in their own lives. You will be blessed, encouraged and motivated in your own efforts to share the Lord by the stories and his example."

Dr. J. Carl Laney
Western Seminary

CONTENTS

The Author's Note   xi

The Empty Seat   xii

1. The Christ Mandate   1
2. The Call to Go Fishing   15
3. The Power Behind Soul Winning   29
4. More Power   43
5. The Power of Prayer behind Evangelism   57
6. Life Message   73
7. NO Spiritual Gift of Evangelism   87
8. Soteriology: The Doctrine of Salvation   105
9. The Role of Faith in Salvation/Invisible Made Visible   121
10. The Spread of the Gospel   137
11. Pathways to Christ's Way   153

Acknowledgments   171

About the Author   173

THE AUTHOR'S NOTE

As you read this book, there are a few things you should know. I am completely blind. I was not always blind, so my stories are from the periods in my life when I could and could not see. This makes no difference to the content of the book, but it may help your understanding while reading these true stories.

In my firsthand accounts, I either changed the names of the individuals being ministered to or left them out entirely. This is because most of them are still living their lives somewhere, and I did not want to place any undo focus on them and their lives. On the flip side, I used real names when speaking of friends and family who are in the life of soul winning themselves, because I felt their ministry of sharing Christ was worth noting. I obtained their permission to do so.

I wrote this book to help Christians who desire to participate more in the Great Commission of Christ. I assume the reader has some prior knowledge of the Christian walk and evangelism because the book is distinctly about the theology of soul winning. The stories I told are for explanation and encouragement, but my aim is to speak to this important area of theology. I know that *The Empty Seat* can also help a local church develop in this area of ministry. I am praying for God's blessing on anyone who takes the time to expand their perspective on salvation by interacting with the theology, scriptures, and true-life stories in this tome.

—Harry Olsen

CHAPTER 1
THE CHRIST MANDATE

The aircraft suddenly lost altitude, then jerked upward and seemed to slide sideways for a while and then started upward again, followed by a steep, white-knuckled drop. A little voice in my spirit said, "Ok, here's your chance." I was on a flight from Portland, Oregon, to Denver, Colorado, sitting next to a seventy-nine-year-old priest named Allen, who was moving to Colorado to retire. He had been in the priesthood of the Catholic Church for fifty-nine years and would retire the next day on his eightieth birthday. For roughly two hours, we talked and joked while I prayed in my soul for an opportunity to share Christ with him and to learn if his eternity was settled. That opportunity had yet to present itself. Turbulence was the norm at Denver International Airport, but this was indeed the worst I had experienced, and it gave me the opportunity I was looking for.

I didn't even think through my next comment because it was the most natural question to bring up. "Allen, if one of these turbulences were to throw us to the ground, and we died, how would you know you were going to Heaven?" He took a turbulent-filled moment to answer. Then he said, "I would just hope I'd played my cards right." He went on to ask, "And, what about you? How would you know?" I paused to think and gather my reply as we bounced around in our seats. I answered that I didn't think it was about religion, his or mine, or anyone else's. I told him I believed it was an issue of surrender to the work of Christ on the Cross as being the only way to the Father. Then I brought up my understanding that his belief system and mine shared the same primary tenant —the atonement of Christ for the sins of anyone who believed. As we continued to bounce and plunge and rise, he thought it over. Then he answered with a distant sound in his voice. "I'm remembering a prayer I haven't thought of for probably fifty years." He named a saint I had never heard of before. He slowly quoted the entire prayer. Then with a new firmness in his voice, he said, "Yes. That's it! Surrendering to Christ's atonement is the only way." I agreed with him. The turbulence ended just before we landed. At the gate, we said our farewells, and I never saw him again.

My priest friend, Allen, sat in what I like to call the *empty seat*. He had been prayed for before he ever stepped foot onto the plane. I believe God sovereignly placed him there in the seat next to me; I had asked God to purposefully put someone in the *empty seat*, someone who needed to hear the gospel, and

He saw fit to honor that prayer. Before I fly, I pray this way, and in recent years, I have flown a lot for ministry purposes.

Throughout this book, I will share stories about the *empty seats* on airplanes, which God has divinely filled for His purposes. But the concept of an *empty seat* speaks to the matter of saving souls in many contexts, not just on planes. This book is ultimately about the *empty seats* in and around your life and mine, which He desires to fill with the newly redeemed. This includes the seat at your dining table that should be filled by that wayward family member, the seat on a train or bus, or a park bench, where a stranger will sit—the one who desperately needs Christ. Ultimately, He desires to fill every seat at the banquet table in His Holy presence. This book is about filling the *empty seats* in our personal lives and in our churches.

As you read *The Empty Seat*, you will learn about what Jesus, the Christ, specifically taught his followers to do. He instructed them to fill the seats at the banquet table in His heavenly home. Jesus' followers, or disciples, were known as "The Way" because they claimed to know the way to God and His Heaven. They were also known as Christians, or "Little Christs," or in other words, little images of Jesus. When they gathered together, they were called "The Church," which means "the called out gathering." All these references were, in some ways, external observations. But the disciples knew, on the inside, what they were called to do because Jesus had been specific with them. He had told them to go throughout the world and make disciples of every ethnicity. Jesus' disciples were even given a geographical plan in the Bible in Acts 1:8. Then Paul prophetically clarified that, together, the disciples were Jesus' body on Earth until He returned to the earth in His resurrected form.

The early Church was clear about its mandate—share Jesus with the world. But now, two thousand years later, His Church has been sidetracked and even co-opted by what I refer to as "religious corporations" for specialized fellowship. In some ways, these corporations or churches are social, feel-good societies, which create their spin on "What would Jesus do?" Others have adopted the feel-good approach of surrendering to a bunker mentality because they believe it is so bad out there in the world that the best the Church can do is hunker down and stay away and stay pure. Such churches are not only losing all their young people, but they are losing the battle. If the Church refuses to follow the biblical mandate and "storm the gates of Hell," it has forgotten the teachings of the New Testament (see Acts 4:19, 20, 29 and Matthew 16:18 – 19).

I want to talk about the clear mandate in the New Testament to internalize, preach, declare, and live the gospel out loud. In 1 Corinthians 12:27, Paul says, "You are the body of Christ and members individually" (NKJV). The *you* in the text has a dual meaning. It speaks of the corporate body and of the individual members that comprise it. The significant point here is that Christ's earthly, physical body is now in its resurrected form, at the right hand of the Father on high, making intercession for us (1 Timothy 2:5 and Colossians 3:1). Because His physical body is no longer here, we are now Christ's body on Earth. Whatever Christ Jesus' priorities were while He was physically on earth automatically transferred to us when He returned to Heaven. That is our mandate, individually and together, to be Christ's body on Earth.

These truths take on power because Jesus Himself explained that we would be occupied with His presence through His Spirit. In John 14: 16-20, the Gospel writer quotes the words of Jesus:

> And I will ask the Father, and he will give you another Helper, to be with you forever, even the Spirit of truth, whom the world cannot receive, because it neither sees him nor knows him. You know him, for he dwells with you and will be in you. I will not leave you as orphans; I will come to you. Yet a little while and the world will see me no more, but you will see me. Because I live, you also will live. In that day you will know that I am in my Father, and you in me, and I in you.

Let me repeat Jesus' words because they are so important: "I am in my Father, and you are in me, and I am in you" (John 14:20). We are the body of Jesus Christ moving through time and place on planet Earth. Jesus is literally in us. Who else does He have?

The world has no Jesus to see if it does not see Jesus in you and me. The world has no Jesus to hear if it does not hear the word of Jesus through you and me. Like Paul says in Romans 10:8b, "The word is near you, in your mouth and in your heart (that is, the word of faith that we proclaim)." Later, in the same chapter, Paul explains that the lost cannot hear unless they are told. Then he wraps up by saying in verse 17, "So faith comes from hearing, and hearing through the word of Christ."

Let me share a story from one of the churches I planted. I was in the educational part of our recently built little building. The church was located in a small town on the southern coast of Oregon. As I walked down the central hallway, I encountered a lady looking around, followed by another lady who looked lost. The first lady said she was looking for the Reverend and seemed surprised when I told her that I was the pastor. I was in my early thirties and didn't look the part of a reverend. She resignedly said, "I need help." And then, pointing to the lady with her, she said, "She needs help! She's my sister from California who's been brought up to me, hoping that the peace and solitude of the area might fix her. She's been to nine therapists, but no one's been able to help her. She's been here almost two weeks, and nothing's changed. She hasn't said a word since she's been here. In fact, it's been a very long time since she's said a word to anyone at all. She's supposed to go home the day after tomorrow. I'm desperate. I thought maybe I should see if religion might help. She's desperate."

Quite frankly, I was too much of a novice pastor in an American church to tell them that I shouldn't be the one to help. You see, I had the rich heritage of growing up in the exciting, power-filled world of dynamic missionary activity. From my teens, I had served and seen Christ's power on display. I invited the sisters into my office and offered them a seat, at which point, the first lady who had spoken with me seated her sister and then said, "I'll be back. Her name is Laura." I assumed she was just going to the restroom, but she darted out of the church to her car and drove away. I sat down on a chair across from Laura. At that time, I still had some sight. Laura sat in the middle of my couch, with her feet tucked up under her, her chin on her chest, and hands in her lap. We sat there in silence while I spoke in my heart to the Great Comforter, Counselor, and Prince of Peace. I asked for direction and wisdom. Obviously, I had no experience to draw from for a situation like this.

I had been told, the first step a counselor takes in the first meeting with a client is to ask questions, and that is what I did. But I received no answers, just profoundly depressed body language. If I hadn't seen Laura walking into the church myself, I would have thought she was comatose.

A thought came into my mind, which I learned was God's way of speaking to me when I was listening, and I was listening intently at that moment. The voice said, "Sing and speak My Words to her." The words of a worship chorus, words that were actually scripture, came into my mind, so I quietly began to sing that song, repeating it a few times. Then I kept going, to another song with scriptural lyrics, which mentioned the Name of Jesus. As a young father, I had learned this method for my infants to find peace as I rocked them to sleep.

Songs with Jesus' Name in them are the very best peace-bringers. Think about the peace and strength in the following lyric, which you may already know:

Jesus, Jesus, Jesus,
There's just something about that Name.

Master, Savior, Jesus,
Like the fragrance after the rain. (Gaither, 1970)

I sang the words of God as Laura sat there. Then I began quoting scripture as it came to my mind. Because I am legally blind, I have memorized a lot of scripture. The scriptures I spoke to Laura spoke of Jesus and about the power in His Name and His goodness, love, and strength. I even told Bible stories. Then the words from the Word that were coming out of me focused on the Cross, and about victory, and about salvation. Finally, my words, which were really His words, ended. There was silence, and with my limited sight, I saw no response from Laura. Instinctively, I knew what the next step at that moment should be. I told her that she could break the power over her, which was the power of darkness, by surrendering to Jesus. I explained to her that I was going to pray to God, and if she felt it in her heart, she should repeat the words she heard me say to God in her heart. I prayed slowly and out loud. I prayed words of surrender to God's eternal plan for salvation through His death on the Cross. As I closed the prayer, I said, "In Jesus' Name, amen." Laura said softly but clearly, "In Jesus' Name, amen."

Her first words in a really long time were, "In Jesus' Name, amen." I did not ask her about her life. Instead, we spoke about Jesus. She had absolutely no background in the faith. She asked. I answered. And she kept asking. It was two and a half hours after Laura first sat down on the empty couch when Laura's sister returned and peered around the opened door. I imagine that her mouth must have dropped open as she saw Laura animatedly asking questions. She sobbed as she dropped down next to Laura on the couch and hugged her.

They cried together for a while on the couch. I wish I knew more about the rest of Laura's story. But after they left my office, I never heard from either of them again. In fact, I never even learned the sister's name. There was no way I could follow up with them. But the words of God's Holy Word, the Bible, spoke through me that day to Laura's heart, and she was saved forever.

My experience with Laura was no surprise to me. While growing up, my dad had often told me of the power of the Word, and of the words that God speaks through any of His willing servants. One of my father's experiences occurred in what was then called the Union of South Africa. It was in the 1950s, and it took place in the most formidable prison in the country, *The Fort,* in the city of Johannesburg. My dad, Marlin Olsen, was a missionary with TEAM Missions. He used to put on his white collar and black dickey, a necessary vestment in that context, and go into prison every Sunday afternoon. The doors to the cells in the awaiting-trial courtyard were opened so prisoners could leave their cells and gather in the courtyard to hear my father preach. Some of the prisoners, however, stayed in their cells and gambled or smoked, generally ignoring the preaching of the Word.

One afternoon, a man named Victor came out of his cells where he had been gambling with matchsticks and followed my dad to the door that exits the courtyard. Victor explained to my dad that as much as he was trying to ignore the preaching, he was drawn by a statement my dad had made. The two of them talked alone in that corner of the awaiting-trial courtyard, and Victor was marvelously saved. Later in this chapter, I will share the unbelievable ending to this story. But to this point, the words of Christ, the Living Word, were taken into that place by God's willing servant, my dad, and spoken. These words became irresistible to that hardened man whom, unbeknownst to my dad, God had been preparing for salvation.

Jesus made the statement about His own ministry mandate in Luke 19:10 by saying that He, the Son of Man, had specifically come to seek out the lost so they could be saved. Jesus said this after He had spoken to Zacchaeus, declaring that salvation had come to that house. In that passage, Jesus stated that His mandate as the Son of Man was to seek and to save the lost. So then, as His flesh and blood body right now, could it really be thought to be different for us? My mandate, your mandate, as well as the mandate of every believer who has lived since the birth of the Church, is to seek and to save that which is lost. In other words, to fill the *empty seat*. This mandate is not a sidebar of church life, like buildings, and programs, and church fun nights, and counting the offering. Jesus' life in His personal flesh body exemplified this every day of His recorded ministry life, right down to His brutal death, burial, and resurrection. He went and sought, and spoke, and loved, and died. As we saw from Romans 10:14, how will they hear without a proclaimer? Can we not see clearly now that it is you and me who are His flesh-and-blood body, His "now-body"?

Allow me to show more examples of Jesus Christ's personal mandate being extended to His disciples and to us. In John 7:37-39, John recorded these comments made by Jesus:

> If anyone thirsts, let him come to me and drink. Whoever believes in me, as the Scripture has said, "Out of his heart will flow rivers of living water." Now this he said about the Spirit, whom those who believed in him were to receive, for as yet the Spirit had not been given, because Jesus was not yet glorified.

Jesus was offering Living Water through His Spirit. This passage tells His followers, then and now, that Living Water would flow out of them when His Spirit would fill them.

In Matthew 10:20, Jesus tells His disciples and us that the Spirit of the Father would speak the message of the gospel through us. Twenty verses later, Jesus goes on to say that if someone receives us, they are receiving Him, as well as He who sent Him. This is more of the unbroken line of the contiguous Church Age mandate. Jesus' flesh-and-blood body is now you and me and every believer in Christ, whether they acknowledge their ongoing mandate or not.

Remember in the advent story that Jesus' own Name indicates saving His people. We are to be witnesses. This is not to do "witness-ey" kinds of things, but to *BE* witnesses. Those two things are quite different. Our role is to be Christ's flesh-and-blood in our world. We are to be about the salvation of people. We are to be about populating Heaven. We are to be about

filling the *empty seats* at the banquet table in His presence.
What a privilege! Yet some treat it as a chore, and others treat
it as if the Bible doesn't really extend this mandate to you and
me. That, I'm afraid, is a cop-out.

Now, here is the rest of Victor's story from *The Fort* in
Johannesburg, South Africa. Several weeks after Victor first
followed my dad to the exit, he followed him there again.
Victor had become a fully devoted disciple of Jesus Christ. His
soul was voraciously eating up every word spoken and written
about Jesus Christ that he could lay his hands on in that place.
He asked for prayer as he told my dad his story, which both
thrilled Dad's heart and terrified him at the same time.

Victor and two other men had been hired to kill a rich
woman's husband. They did the deed, were paid, and then got
caught. They were clearly guilty of first-degree murder. They
had, of course, said they were not guilty. His problem became
evident when Victor reminded my dad that during the previous
week while preaching, my dad had told the prisoners God
cannot bless a lie.

That coming week, on Thursday, Victor and the other two
men were to have their plea hearing. Victor told my dad that he
could no longer tell a lie about what had happened. He said he
was going to plead guilty. The punishment for his crime was
hanging, so Victor asked for prayer.

My dad told me he barely slept that week, knowing that
Victor was putting a noose around his own neck. On Thursday,
my dad was one of the first people to enter the courtroom.
The room filled up because Victor's was a high-profile case in

Johannesburg. The prosecution entered and took their seats at their table. At that time in South African history, the prosecution was known as "The Crown." The defense came in, followed by the three accused men. Victor was defendant number three.

The overview of the murder case and its classification as first-degree murder, with an arbitrary sentence of hanging by the neck until dead, was announced by The Crown prosecution. The judge asked defendant number one how he pled, and he said he was not guilty. He asked defendant number two how he pled, and he, too, pled not guilty.

By this time, my dad said he ceased to breathe as he prayed for strength for Victor who would surely be executed if he changed his plea to guilty. The judge went on to ask defendant number three how he pled. Victor, with a strong and clear voice, said, "Guilty as charged, your Honor." There was a shocked murmur in the courtroom followed by tense silence. The Crown prosecution looked at each other, then down at their paperwork, then at Victor, then at the judge, then conferred again with each other.

Finally, the lead prosecutor stood up and said, "The Crown has no case against defendant number three." Shocked murmur filled the courtroom, followed by a growing ripple of excited realization about the significance of what The Crown's words meant. An equally amazed judge told the guards to release defendant number three. Victor didn't know what to do, so he walked out down the center aisle, followed by my teary-eyed dad. Both defendants, number one and two, had a lengthy trial, after which they were found guilty of first-degree murder. They were hanged.

Being a part of Christ's now-body is a great adventure, and filling the *empty seat*, as well as being the occupant of the *empty seat*, can be an adventure too.

CHAPTER 2
THE CALL TO GO FISHING

I've only been fishing once in my life. My grandfather, who I was named after, took my brother and me fishing as small boys on the banks of the Columbia River in Washington State. He baited our hooks and cast out into the river for us, explaining each step as he went. Then he stuck devices in the sand at an angle, facing the river, and put our poles into them. He put bells on the end of our rods and told us to watch for the pole to jiggle and the bell to ring. I was so excited. This was fishing, and I was with my beloved Grandpa Harry. I watched and watched, and listened and listened. I waited and watched and listened. The pole did not jiggle, and the bell never rang. That was my first and last time going fishing.

I tell you this to emphasize that even though I am writing this chapter about fishing for souls, I really know nothing about fishing, other than what I have observed or heard from the fishing tales of other guys. However, my limited education about fishing has made me realize that, for the most part, fishing is a planned activity and often involves a lot of work.

A shuttle bus driver at Denver International Airport helped me clearly understand this point. It was 4:30 a.m. in the morning. My wife Carol and I were on this shuttle because we had an early flight to catch. Since we were the only passengers on the shuttle that Monday morning, I engaged the driver in small talk, and he told Carol and me about his life. It turned out he was an avid fisherman. He had just been on a fishing trip the previous Saturday. He described getting up at 3:00 a.m. and driving with his buddy for an hour and a half into the mountains. They parked their vehicle and proceeded to hike an hour and a half more to a favorite fishing hole. His musings became almost ecstatic as he shared about the size of the fish they had caught. Then he described how he and his bud always left enough time to hike back out before dark, so they could drive home. In my naiveté, I commented that they must have had a feast the next day. He smiled and said, "Nope...we threw them all back into the water." He explained that they didn't really like eating fish and disliked cleaning them even more. The salient point I learned and am trying to bring out here is that fishing is very intentional. It doesn't happen by accident. It is done for a purpose.

Now that I am such an "expert" on fishing, I have drawn a conclusion about what Peter and Andrew and James and John would have understood when Jesus said to them, "Follow me and I will make you fishers of men" (from Matt. 4:18-22). I believe they would have understood that what they were under-taking with Jesus would be intentional, require thought, get messy, and include much work and maybe even danger. This was a call to action with adventure and great reward.

In Matthew 10, Jesus sends His twelve disciples out with what we can call "fishing instructions." They were not just to go and hang out in different towns, but to engage people and communities wherever they went. Jesus gave them instruction, along with powerful bait for catching nets full of souls for the kingdom of God. He did this yet again with seventy-two others seen in Luke 10, stating those famous words in verse 2, "And he said to them, 'the harvest is plentiful, but the laborers are few. Therefore, pray earnestly to the Lord of the harvest to send out laborers into his harvest'." This mixes metaphors, fishing with farming, but it is the same principle of being intentional and going out for the purpose of gathering souls for the Kingdom. Remember what I just said in the previous paragraph, that what they were undertaking with Jesus would be intentional, and require thought, getting messy, much work, and maybe even danger?

Since I am already mixing metaphors, think of the sower that Jesus spoke of in Matthew 13. He could never have sown his seed while sitting at home or hanging out at the Synagogue. Sowing seed was intentional and labor-intensive. In the same way, Jesus told other parables to help us see the drive to seek souls, including the story of the shepherd and the lost sheep and the woman with the lost coin in Luke 15:4-10. I could go on and on, showing this pattern of intentionality, but the passion

and intentionality and labor intensity of ministering the gospel
of Jesus Christ is overwhelmingly evident in the Gospels. We
see it in Jesus' actions both while in His own flesh and blood
body, and in His teachings and instructions.

A number of years ago, I was in Salem, Oregon, for a
statewide church conference. My wife was not able to be with
me, so I carpooled with three pastors from my area. On the full
day of the conference, my friends decided to get in the car we
all came in and go get fast food during the lunch break. I did
not want to go because my heart was a little heavy thinking
about a thousand skilled Christians in the conference
surrounded by a city of thousands of people headed for a
Christ-less eternity. I told them I would not be going with them
but thanked them for the invitation. Then I walked into town
praying in my soul for an opportunity to share Christ. I went
fishing.

I prayed and prayed and walked and looked for a person
wearing a sandwich board saying something like, "Talk to me
about Jesus because I am going to Hell." That person, if they
existed, must have been on a different street because I did not
encounter them. Instead, I went into a large old building, which
had been converted into a mini-mall with indoor stores. Finally,
I found an elderly lady sitting on a bench inside the mall. I
thought I had found my opportunity to share Christ. I went
and sat down and tried to engage her in conversation. She got
this frightened look on her face, stood up, and darted away
from me into a nearby store. I guess I did not have a benevo-
lent, pastoral look.

Disappointed, I wandered down a couple of blocks, crossed the street, and was about to give up. I thought I must have misunderstood what God had said to my soul. Just then, I noticed a café coming up. I decided to go in. It turned out to be a bustling lunchtime eatery. The hostess informed me that there were no available tables, but if I was ok with it, there was one *empty seat* at the counter. Since the lunch break at the conference was short, I took the seat; I sat between a lady on the left and a man on my right.

By God's organizational plan, I ended up in conversation with the man. Allow me to abbreviate what was a long story. He ended up telling me he had lived on the east side of Portland, which was over fifty miles away. He worked in downtown Portland in the music field as a music producer. That morning, he had left for work at the usual time, but with a heavy heart, and before he realized it, he had totally missed the downtown exits. Discouraged and wondering if he had the guts to end his own life, he decided to keep driving. Finally, he became aware that he had no plan and was wasting time, so he chose to pull off at the Salem exit and turn around. Still distracted, he became lost and found himself on a street downtown in front of an eatery and surprisingly hungry.

At that moment, I knew I had heard God's prompting correctly. Through lunch and multiple cups of coffee afterward, I talked with Ron, my God-arranged encounter. He told me he knew he needed what we were discussing, and then he quietly prayed with me to surrender to Christ's saving work. He was deeply moved and quite encouraged to discover God had arranged his whole day, right up to that seat at that counter, for his own personal, divine encounter, which God had designed just for him. The time came when Ron knew that he had to head back to Portland to go to work. We exchanged information, and I told him I would have a pastor who ministered in his area call him. He left, and I looked around and saw that the café had emptied out.

After Ron walked off, the only one left at the counter in the café was the lady to the left of me with whom I hadn't exchanged one word. Right then, she turned to me with an emotional catch in her voice and told me that she was an out of fellowship Christian who knew, as soon as Ron and I began to talk, that she was meant to be there at that moment. While I was explaining Christ to Ron, she was renewing her relationship with Christ. In her heart, she became aware that God had work for her to do as well, right then and right there. She knew she was participating in a God-event at that counter on that day because she strongly felt a call to pray and stay at the eatery until the work of salvation in Ron's life was complete. She would be very late getting back from lunch, and so would I, but neither of us cared. We prayed together for her and Ron's new life in Christ and then went our way. That afternoon in Salem, Oregon, I had gone fishing intentionally. As it turned out, God had prepared an exceptional fishing hole for two believers that afternoon, with an extraordinary catch.

In my observation, fishing for souls is talked about a great deal but engaged in less and less by individuals and churches. I believe there are several reasons for this. There are churches that have become internally focused on the grind of church growth and on trying to serve their people demonstrably better than the church up the road serves theirs. This competitiveness, which few churches will admit to, is subconsciously present in most conversations about one's church, leaving one to ask questions like:

- Are there enough programs?
- Maybe we need to do more than just stream the service?
- Maybe our church also needs a TV or radio program?
- Maybe be we need more advertising. After all, aren't we in friendly competition for souls with other churches by trying to produce the most impressive Christmas and Easter services?

All of this can become a real rat race. None of these things are bad in and of themselves, but the motives, attitude, and behavior are often because of churches taking on a business model, which steals time and energy from the Church's Great Commission. We forget to, as they say, make the main thing the main thing. The Church is never mandated to grow but to *make disciples*. 1 Corinthians 3 says that God brings the growth.

Both the internal workings of the church growth movement's race to the top, and the community events that it demands, take work. What's sad is, in the long run, even when these are public community events, too often, they are not actually evangelistic. Perhaps, many churches are fishing for growth and just *hoping* for the salvation of souls. An event with bouncy toys, soft-serve ice cream, music bands, and face painting is a lot of work, and may, with good advertising, bring people from the community onto a church's property. But in some cases, if not most, such events yield little or no actual meaningful growth in regular attendance and few salvations. Seldom is a person coming onto the church's property for fun and games the same as an actual salvific contact unless someone intentionally engages with them while they are there and gets contact information. Often, this kind of intentionality is not planned into the event. A personal invitation must be intentionally made, or the recreational visit to the church property will probably never become a fruitful contact.

If intentional outreach creates meaningful contacts, they need to be followed up on. This is when the hard work begins and where many churches drop the ball. Ultimately, an intentional, fun event like this is not harmful, except for possibly using up the passion and energy of volunteers and usually depleting limited resources. But I can say this, most likely, an event such as this will have little or no value for people being saved without intentional mechanisms being built-in for exposing the church's guests to the claims of Christ. It might fill an *empty seat* in the church building but often not fill a seat at the feast table in Heaven.

Surprisingly, I hear church leaders repeatedly say that direct contact with event visitors shouldn't be pursued because it could be perceived as being invasive. What's a church supposed to do? Unfortunately, many churches choose to do nothing. A church must understand there is no way to make contacts that could lead to changed lives without honest and creative thinking. They must think about cultural opportunities for direct engagement, followed by intentional action. We are not trying to build our own churches, but Christ's Church. He is God, and His truth-teaching Helper, the Counselor, the Holy Spirit, lives in us. Surely, He, the Spirit of Christ Himself, knows how to make the kind of contacts that will lead to individuals becoming His disciples from any walk of life. He will intervene in culture and community to make the work of His body possible. The local church people must pray, and research community sources, and think, and make a divinely guided plan, and did I mention pray? Then, they must follow through on that plan until it is complete. This is work, but it is work with reward. Remember, God is not willing that any should perish.

Even a person like me, someone completely ignorant about fishing, knows that because there are different fish in different bodies of water, fishermen need many varieties of skills, and lures, and equipment bait, and favorable conditions to catch a meaningful catch. This is equally clear for local church evangelism. Often, local churches work hard but end up doing ineffective labor. Sometimes, they are doing what they have read or heard that some other church, in some other place, did with some effect. They figure, "If it worked for them, it will work for us too." This is not necessarily true. No matter where the church is located, no matter what the neighborhood may be like, God has within that church every person with the specific gifts He needs to accomplish the next step in the life of that church, according to His specific plan for that church. If another church's plan is being pursued, the plan may fall short because the other church had a different neighborhood and different gifting in that church.

In a later chapter, I will lay out proven powerful pathways that a church can create to draw people in to hear the claims of Christ. No, these are not business plans but plans from the scripture. God is way capable of helping any local church, anywhere, if the church prays for wisdom and then applies that wisdom to develop a plan on how that church can reach its own community. We pray because His ways are higher than ours (Isa. 55:9). Fishing for souls as a local church needs to be prayerfully planned and intentionally executed if it is to result in a divine catch. One thing that is always true, whether it involves an individual, or a local church, or an association of churches, or the foreign mission field, is this: prayed-up people who are intentionally following a divinely inspired plan for evangelism, *are* fishing for souls. Remember, it is God's job to fill the nets as He sees fit.

There is a wonderfully true story from central India, which happened in the early 2000s. In a city of about four million people that had absolutely no Christian witness, the mighty power of God was released as a group of God's people became intentional about fishing for souls. A group of church planters from India had been called out and trained earlier by my older brother Ted and his associates from his ministry to unreached people groups. He had brought together these leaders for the purpose of committing to clearly preach the gospel in every people group, resulting in at least one effective church in each one. These Indian men went into this city and intentionally targeted this unreached people group. They had been trained in a similar approach that Jesus used with His twelve disciples and the seventy-two He sent out (Matthew 10 and Luke 10). They were given the same kind of fishing instructions.

These Indian teams went into that city and went from house to house, looking for a person of peace and offering to pray for the sick in that house and pray for other problems they might have. There were healings that took place while doing this. Hindus have millions of idols they call gods, so they were not averse to hearing about what they thought was just another god named Jesus. But even with the healings, they were still satisfied with their primary religious focus, which was an ancient dead spiritual leader and the temple they had built in his honor. This temple was central to their life. A statue of the spiritual leader, in his honor, sat in the midst of the temple, with two tall spires on each side which towered over the temple. The worship of this dead leader was led by a priestess. The clincher of the efficaciousness of this brand of religion was a pure and freshwater spring that bubbled up by the temple. People came from miles around for water from that spring. Pure water in much of India is considered to be a treasure of great worth.

The church planters made it their daily practice to prayer-walk through the city before they began house to house ministry. Each day, they circled the temple in their prayer walk. Sound familiar? If not, see Hebrews 11:30 relating to the walls of

Jericho. For many days, they ministered with negligible results, but they soldiered on, ministering from house to house and praying while walking through different parts of the city. Every day included walking around the temple, but still, there were no breakthroughs. This continued daily for a week or more until one day, the spiritual walls began to crumble. After having prayed and walked for those many days, when the church planters entered the city on that final day, they found the community somewhat in an uproar. People were rushing franticly toward the temple. The church planters followed them and found dismay everywhere. The people were in shock.

During the night, without even a tremor of an earthquake, the towering spires on either side of the temple had fallen toward each other and landed on the top of the temple. The temple was utterly crushed. The larger-than-life-sized idol, which was their object of worship, was destroyed. Added to this, the people found the temple's bubbling spring of clean water had dried up. They searched for their priestess and discovered her body where a leopard had killed her and left her sari, her outer garment, hanging over a tree branch.

In one night, their main deity and religious worship were nullified completely. From that day on, people earnestly wanted to know about the Almighty God named Jesus. Several churches now thrive among this formally unreached people group of central India. My brother Ted, on a later trip to India, went to see for himself if what he had been told was true. He found that the temple had not been rebuilt. Instead, the people had poured a concrete slab over the rubble. Where the bubbling spring had been was now just a stagnant pond with garbage floating in it. Ted saw that a part of the priestess' sari was still dangling from the tree branch. And by the way, the spring of fresh, pure, bubbling water had now mysteriously resurfaced outside of the city and was being enjoyed by all.

Let's think again through this kind of intentionality resulting in fishermen pulling in full nets. What if my brother Ted had not gone to India, and what if the native church leaders from central India had not been open to the challenge to go after this unreached people group? What if they had not been willing to be trained and then go knock on doors, and pray, and persevere? Catching one soul or a net full of people doesn't happen by accident. Let's obey Jesus and go fishing. Dare I repeat myself? Going fishing with Jesus will need to be intentional, require thought, much work, messiness, and maybe even danger.

Over the years, I have preached a message of comparing cruise ships to fishing boats. Let's say a cruise ship has two thousand people aboard. Most likely, 20 percent of the people aboard would be the crew who did all the work. The other 80 percent would be cruisers who were pampered and spoiled. I planted churches on coastlines and waterways, and there were commercial fishermen in three of the churches my wife and I started. I learned from them that on a fishing vessel, there are no cruisers expecting to be pampered. In many instances, if a sailor is not pulling their weight, they are taken to the nearest port and put off the vessel. Every sailor is paid a percentage of the catch, so no one can kick back.

American churches can be a lot like either one of these, a cruise ship or a fishing boat. Jesus made it quite clear which one He intends for us, His disciples, to be when He told the sets of brothers to follow Him, and He would make them fishers of men (Mark 1:16-20). Jesus said of Himself, "For even the Son of Man came not to be served but to serve, and to give his life a ransom for many" (Mark 10:45).

For the ship in my metaphor to be a fishing vessel, not only must each individual aboard decide what kind of sailor he or she is, a cruiser or a fisher-of-men, but the vessel they are on will create the context to move and direct the sailor to be either one or the other. What kind of seaman are you? And what kind is your church? A cruise ship or a fishing vessel?

CHAPTER 3

THE POWER BEHIND SOUL WINNING

We know that Jesus, in His resurrected body, "...has gone into Heaven and is at the right hand of God, angels and authorities and powers, having been made subject to Him" (1 Pet. 3:22 NKJV).

We also know that "Jesus Christ is the same yesterday and today and forever" (Heb. 13:8). Given those things, we shouldn't be surprised when the apostle Paul says, "For the kingdom of God does not consist in talk but in power" (1 Cor. 4:20).

What should surprise us is that so many churches and individuals lead such spiritually impotent lives. The scriptures scream the power of God reaching down through people.

For example, Ephesians 3:16b says, "...strengthened with power through his Spirit in your inner being." And verse 20 says, "Now to him who is able to do far more abundantly than all that we ask or think, according to the power at work within us."

If Paul's word is not enough, Mark said about Jesus, "...and He began to send them out two by two and gave them power..." (6:7 NKJV). Paul makes this concept easier for us to understand in Philippians 4:13, where he states, "I can do all things through him who strengthens me." 2 Corinthians 10:3-4 adds more:

> For though we walk in the flesh, we are not waging war according to the flesh. For the weapons of our warfare are not of the flesh but have divine power to destroy strongholds.

In Mark 12:24, Jesus spoke these words in the form of a question, which the Pharisees would be forced to think about, "Jesus said to them, 'Is this not the reason you are wrong, because you know neither the Scriptures nor the power of God?'"

I believe it wasn't just the Pharisees of old who needed to hear Jesus say these words. You and I, as believers, along with our churches, also need to hear this powerful statement of truth from Jesus Christ. Jesus is also saying to us, the somewhat weakened Church of today: "Is this not the reason you are wrong, because you know neither the scriptures nor the power of God?"

The stories in this chapter may catch you off guard. Sadly, today's Church has somehow forgotten the divine power and strength given to us by the Spirit to destroy strongholds (2 Cor.10:4). God wants us to expect this power in our daily lives as we allow Him to work in and through us. It is *HIS* power, not ours, that is promised to every believer. I pray these stories will excite you, not confuse you. They are true, and it is God who gets the glory.

It might be true that my brother Ted, my sister Mary Beth, and I had a head start in understanding the things I have been sharing in this book because we had the blessing of being missionary kids. You see, our mom and dad, Marlin and Gladys Olsen, were missionaries in Africa during our youth. As a child, my dad became my superhero. I recall at least two times when he came home with the windows of his Willys Jeep shot out after ministering in the rough neighborhoods of Johannesburg. Both times, the trajectories of the entry and exit points of the bullets demonstrated they should have passed right through my dad. To me, as a little guy, this meant that his God, my God, gave my dad superpowers. I shudder in retrospect to think what our godly mother must have felt and thought during these times of bullet-shattered windows.

A few years later, in our early teens, Ted, MaryBeth, and I saw a neighborhood open wide to the gospel due to a well-known and influential matriarch of the community. She had cancer in her abdomen and was sent home to die, but she was prayed for and was miraculously healed from cancer. Given the power behind the gospel, this no longer surprised us. Once again, later in our teens, we heard that a town official had died unexpectedly of natural causes. He had opposed a church being planted in the neighborhood and specifically made it known, insistently, that he opposed the gospel being preached by a white man, my dad, in a non-white community. My parents had been praying for God to open up that community for the gospel, in whatever way He had planned. So, no, it didn't feel strange when this man suddenly died because he consistently opposed the gospel. The power of God for the gospel, well, it is the power of God.

My brother and sister and I knew then, and still believe, that God demonstrates power when asked for and expected by and through those who minister the gospel. I speak of this to help lift your personal expectations of the same God. We grew up expecting to see God's power demonstrated in our lives just as we had the privilege of seeing it played out in our parent's lives, as they lived out and proclaimed the gospel of Jesus Christ. Do not get me wrong, darkness can and does demonstrate power through the appetites of the flesh, through the pull of the world, and often very tangibly through demons or the Devil. But let me remind you that the Devil is just one demon that can only be in one place at one time. And, according to the scriptures, demons and the Devil are outnumbered two to one by the heavenly hosts (see Rev. 12:3-4), leaving the believer-warrior concretely backed up and empowered by God. Now that should get you excited!

When I was ten or eleven in the City of Durban, South Africa, I keenly remember an East Indian family, the Jacobs family. The Jacobs joined one of the churches my dad planted during that term in Africa. This couple, and their son Albert, had come to know Christ out of Hinduism, and the family matured toward living a Christian family life. But despite the change, somehow the Jacobs' daughter, Kitty, never made a personal profession of faith in Christ.

One night, my dad was called to the Jacobs' home in the middle of the night. Kitty was demonstrating violence and extreme physical power. Even though she was a small girl, her father and older brother could not restrain her. My dad found her writhing on the ground like a snake, making hissing snake sounds. It became evident that Kitty was demon-possessed. Dad dealt with her and the family in the same way as he had dealt with other demon possessions he had encountered as a missionary, but the violence toward her family and herself did not abate. Finally, Dad turned to the parents and asked if there was any dedicated Hindu relic still present in the home that had not been removed with all their previous household Hindu shrines after the family received Christ, as would normally have been the practice.

Mrs. Jacobs sheepishly turned to her husband and spoke to him in Hindi. He looked anguished and told my dad that some golden nails had been left above the doors of the house, where they had always been. They explained that these golden nails were dedicated to a Hindu god for good luck.

Immediately, the Jacobs knew what had to happen. They began removing each golden nail and took them outside, and put them in the trash. When they came back into the house, they thought their daughter was dead. Kitty was lying so still. But after praying with her, claiming the power of Jesus's blood, they helped her to her feet, and later that day, when she had rested and eaten, she received the Savior of her soul. The demon possession never happened again. It was the divine power destroying strongholds.

The Devil and his demons can manifest something that looks like power, but that power is subdued by the Name of Christ and attention to His blood that He shed on the Cross. It is true, however, that the flesh can exert power over the body and soul. We see this so clearly in addictions. This pull of the flesh and the world has done much damage to the youth in our Christian families and churches.

But the power that God gives us as an asset of our faith can break down every stronghold for anyone who desires deliverance. So often, we as Christians cower behind any excuse we can find as we move from defeat to defeat. This ought not to be so.

Undeniably, as the children of God, we have: the power of the indwelling Spirit of God, the power of Christ's blood, the power of His Name, the power of the Word, the power of prayer, the power of the gospel itself, and on top of all this, we have angels, and the omnipotent, ever-present Living God. Can I hear an "Amen!"? As the apostle Paul said:

If God is for us, who can be against us? For I am sure that neither death nor life, nor angels nor rulers, nor things present nor things to come, nor powers, nor height nor depth, nor anything else in all creation, will be able to separate us from the love of God in Christ Jesus our Lord. (Romans 8:31, 38, 39)

Now, let's talk about this multifaceted power behind the gospel. I will address two facets of this power in this chapter and the rest in the following chapters. I will be cluster-bombing the chapters with scripture because it's so important to know that this isn't my word but entirely God's Word. Even so, I will only quote a fraction of the many scripture passages that show six facets of the power behind the gospel.

Power of the Indwelling Holy Spirit

The power of the indwelling Holy Spirit is clearly stated by Luke in Acts 1:8, "But you will receive power when the Holy Spirit has come upon you, and you will be my witnesses...." The apostle John, in his first letter, states you, "... have overcome them, for he who is in you is greater than he who is in the world" (1 John 4:4). John said this about the Holy Spirit in his earlier book, the Gospel of John, "And when he comes, he will convict the world concerning sin and righteousness and judgment" (John 16:8). These verses show the Spirit on and in the believer, and we see Him working in the not-yet believers, too, preparing them for the gospel.

A few years ago, Carol and I were flying from Denver to Phoenix. For some reason, instead of a direct flight, we took a flight that stopped in Albuquerque, New Mexico, to drop off and pick up passengers. On the first leg of the journey, the *empty seat* was filled by a disinterested lady who napped. The lady was by the window, so Carol sat beside her, and I sat on the end of the row. In Albuquerque, the lady deplaned, and a man boarded and took this lady's now *empty seat*. Carol skillfully engaged this man, Ben, in conversation, and soon the discussion opened up about his search for God. By the time we were at altitude, Carol had brought me into the conversation. Ben was a Navaho Indian gentleman and a general contractor. He worked all over the country, building a certain type of educational facility. When he was a young adult, he had started doubting what he called the "Indian religion." Later, Ben left the religion and became a Mormon. He saw significant similarities between the two religions, but he liked that Mormonism was better defined and organized than his old faith. But several years as a Mormon had left him feeling empty and wondering about who the true God really was.

The Holy Spirit had convicted Ben of sin, righteousness, and judgment before he ever got on that flight. I believe our prayer for the occupant of that *empty seat* resulted in him being there for the harvest of his soul. He eagerly embraced Christ to fill the emptiness in his soul. The true Spirit of God had drawn a seeking soul to a willing couple on a flight. In fifty-five minutes, from wheels up to wheels down, the occupant of the *empty seat* became a forever-child of the Living God. What if Carol hadn't intentionally engaged Ben in conversation to test his readiness for the gospel? The first occupant of that *empty seat* was just a placeholder for Ben. We must remember and trust that the Spirit is intensely engaged in our ambassadorship for Christ.

In the late 1950s, in South Africa, a lady named Marjorie became a great mother of the faith and of the church near

Durban. She, too, was prepared by the Holy Spirit for salvation in a rather unusual way. On the other hand, my dad was led by the Spirit in his usual way, which was the obedience of faith. On a Sunday afternoon, my dad, as was his practice, was going from home to home in that very tough-toward-the-gospel community. He encountered slammed doors and a few well-placed angry dogs as he obeyed the "fishing instructions" he was led by the Holy Spirit to follow. Remember, Christ's Spirit still knows where the fish are, just like He showed the disciples on two occasions in the Gospels.

Approaching one of the houses in the middle of the block, my dad prayed for strength because so much rejection had made him weary. He knocked on the door, heard nothing at first, and thought this could well be another kind of passive rejection. But before he could turn away, he heard shuffling behind the door. A middle-aged lady with a crippled foot opened the door. Her eyes widened as she saw who it was. She said in English, "Stay there! We've been waiting for you." Then, she shuffled down the hallway as fast as she could and returned with her mother, Marjorie, whose face lit up with excitement. Marjorie repeated what her daughter had just said to my dad. "We have been waiting for you!" Then she asked my dad to follow her. She and her daughter led my dad into a small sitting room and asked him to take a seat. The story they told absolutely describes how the Spirit of God goes before those who bring the Good News.

For many consecutive nights, Marjorie had dreamed the same dream. She saw a large white man with a bald head coming to her door with "the answer." She now said to him, since she now knew his name, "Brother Olsen, what is that answer?" Because my dad was out fishing for souls, he knew just exactly what that answer was. Over the next few weeks, that entire household was marvelously saved. And a church was born in that community, where folks came to meet in that home every Sunday, for months to hear the gospel preached by a large white man with a bald head who followed the Spirit to where God might have prepared a fishing hole. Without going into too much detail, let me just say this: many generations of Marjorie's family have followed Christ faithfully, and the leadership for the nationwide movement of churches and theological institutions came out of that household as well. The Spirit of the One who seeks and saves the lost is still alive and well. He is looking for those who will follow Him to those He has prepared or is preparing for salvation.

The Power of the Cross and the Shed Blood of Christ

The power of the Cross and the shed blood of Christ were seen powerfully in the story earlier in this chapter, through the account of the girl released from demons. The scripture says in 1 Corinthians 1:18, "For the word of the cross is folly to those who are perishing, but to us who are being saved it is the power of God."

The cross is a terrible wooden structure with no power of its own. However, it becomes a powerful symbol of victory as Paul spells out in Colossians 2:13-15:

And you, who were dead in your trespasses and the uncircumcision of your flesh, God made alive together with him, having forgiven us all our trespasses, by canceling the record of debt that stood against us with its legal demands. This he set aside, nailing it to the cross. He disarmed the rulers and authorities and put them to open shame, by triumphing over them in him.

The Cross gets its power from the blood of Jesus, the Son of Man, the Son of God. It was Jesus who fulfilled countless prophesies and types when His blood was splattered all over it and ran down its sides and soaked up the ground. So, the power of the Cross is the power of the blood of Jesus, the Christ.

May I remind you that the scripture explains that the blood of Jesus has freed us from our sins (Revelation 1:5)? Romans 5:9 says that we have been justified by His blood. In Ephesians 1:7, Paul tells us that we have redemption through His blood, the forgiveness of our sins. Colossians 1:20 says that Christ gives us peace by the blood of His cross. The list of powerful changes that Christ has accomplished in our lives through the blood of His cross goes on. His powerful blood helps embattled believers embrace the already accomplished victory and straighten their shoulders and stand up tall, fully equipped with the armor of God. In dark and dangerous moments, the Christian soldier of the faith experiences a powerful boost by the mere mention of Satan's defeat wrought by the blood of Christ on the Cross.

Many years ago, on a Sunday night, my six-year-old daughter and I were locking up the church before heading home. My little girl, Rebekah, pointed to a covered area with picnic tables and told me there was a girl sitting by herself in the dark. As we walked over to her, we saw the "girl" was actually a fifteen-year-old boy with very long hair. To keep to the point I want to make, I will abbreviate his story. This boy, Edgar, was the product of a terrible past, which eventually led to his life as a male prostitute on the streets of Hollywood. He had come to the point of desperation and was sitting at that picnic table, trying to figure out how to get over the top of a fence on a nearby freeway overpass. His plan was to jump into traffic in front of a semi-truck to end what he had decided was his miserable life.

We took him home with us. Edgar became a part of our household and family life, on and off again, until he was twenty-two. Early in his time with us, my friend and I led him to a saving relationship with Christ, but it was through a pitched spiritual battle, a battle where the mere mention of Christ's blood saved the day and Edgar's soul. Let me tell you what happened.

My friend I mentioned above, Jack, was a young man I was discipling. On this particular day, Jack and I were sitting in the living room of the parsonage of the church, on the campus where my daughter and I had found Edgar on the bench just a few days before. Edgar was in the same room with us. We began explaining to him what being a Christian was. It was then that we noticed Edgar was starting to get agitated. As time passed, his agitation escalated, and he grew belligerent with an authoritative voice, a voice we hadn't heard before. For some time,

Edgar would transition back and forth between how we knew him to normally act and this belligerent and increasingly angry person. For everything we said, he had a seemingly prepared, scoffing answer.

By this point, I realized we were at war with an evil spirit. Jack and I noticed that Edgar, when he was aware and in reality, did not even seem to know that he was arguing with us. In addition to this, as his agitation grew, we saw that his head would snap back and forth from looking at us when he was aware and acting normal, to looking away from us when he was acting belligerent, and his voice would change. At last, during one of the times when Edgar was calmer and seemed to be back, in reality, I told him that we were in a battle for his soul with a devil that was in him. Edgar didn't seem to be surprised because he had experienced that kind of darkness before. After this, when the agitator of his soul would speak, it would mock us, but when Edgar mellowed and came back to himself, we would keep speaking the truth to him. By now, he was beginning to be quite frightened.

Finally, in a moment while he was cognizant, I said his name and asked him, "Edgar, do you want Jesus Christ to save you from this and save your soul?" He cried out that he did. The demon snatched him back one more time, but at last, after releasing him again for a moment, I told Edgar to cry out to Jesus, to tell Jesus that he believed in His blood that can cover everyone's sins. Edgar did it. The next attempt to snatch his soul didn't happen. The blood of Christ had freed him. I explained to him what God had just done in his life, and then

Jack and I put our hands on Edgar and prayed for him, claiming the victory over dark forces through the blood of the Lamb. This young man who wanted to kill himself not long before was now saved from Hell and free from demons!

It is true that Edgar still carried significant baggage from the years of living in darkness, and sometimes it was a rough go with him, but the point here is that the blood of Christ broke the power of demons over a troubled young man so that he could never again be possessed by an evil spirit. The Spirit of God was now in his spirit. In retrospect, just as I shuddered for my mom and what she went through on the mission field, I shudder to think of my dear wife, who shared a family life over the years with troubled souls like Edgar, who lived in our home. God was always faithful, though. We never felt that our children were in danger. God never says that entering into the battle for a soul is easy, but He promises to be with us in the struggle. Our children grew up believing in the power of God. We always told our children that the people God brought into our home were "diamonds in the rough."

In this chapter, I have written about the power of God for the work of salvation in general, and specifically the work of the Holy Spirit that is in play because of being a child of God. I mentioned the power that saved our souls and is at work to save souls as we stand up in the battle. Of course, that is the blood of the Cross of Jesus Christ. In the next chapter, we move toward the power that we can effectively wield as a weapon in the warfare that we are in.

CHAPTER 4

MORE POWER

In the previous chapter, we approached the power behind evangelism. We looked first at the broad picture and then focused on two specific facets: the power of the Holy Spirit and the Cross and the blood of Jesus Christ. What I have observed is that *both* facets are intrinsic to being effective in the process of evangelism. The principal value to the believer is to know about the existence of these powers in their lives and believe in the power behind them. The remaining four facets of the power behind evangelism are also actual weapons used in the battle. Let me show you what I mean. Let's begin with the Name of the Lord Jesus Christ.

The Power of the Name of the Lord Jesus Christ

Looking at the big picture first, let me lead off with

Matthew's statement about Jesus. "And in his name the Gentiles will hope" (Matt 12:21). Biblically, His Name contains every description of every power, character, and asset ever ascribed to Jesus. In short, His Name is everything He is described to be. Everything that we could ever hope for. Paul describes the absoluteness of the power and authority of the Name of Jesus in Philippians 2:9-11:

> Therefore, God has highly exalted him and bestowed on him the name that is above every name, so that at the name of Jesus every knee should bow, in heaven and on earth and under the earth, and every tongue confess that Jesus Christ is Lord, to the glory of God the Father.

We are led to understand then that His Name has all power and authority. His name gives anyone and everyone access to eternal life. Here is an example in his Gospel, as John states, "But to all who did receive him, who believed in his name, he gave the right to become children of God" (John 1:12). And Paul says in Romans 10:13, "For 'everyone who calls on the name of the Lord will be saved.'"

"But wait," (as TV ads would say) "there's more!" In the book of Acts, we see the Name of Jesus used in spiritual battle and ministry of healing. "Paul, having become greatly annoyed, turned and said to the spirit, 'I command you in the name of Jesus Christ to come out of her.' And it came out that very hour" (Acts 16:18b). And in Acts 3:6, Peter said, "I have no silver and gold, but what I do have I give to you. In the name of Jesus

Christ of Nazareth, rise up and walk!" Again, in verse 16, "And his name-- by faith in his name-- has made this man strong whom you see and know...."

The scripture in Acts describes the healing of the beggar who was born crippled. I believe and can say with confidence— because I have seen this for myself—that speaking the Name of the Lord Jesus Christ is a powerful weapon; it is as powerful today as it was when Paul or Peter used it in their battles centuries ago.

When I was a senior in boarding school in South Africa, a classmate and I would go out on Sunday afternoons and give out Bibles, and speaking Afrikaans, we would share Christ in the African villages called *Kraals*. We also visited the government townships where the housing was predominantly corrugated Quonset buildings that had been turned into duplexes, with entryways located on both ends. Between the dirt street and the hut, there was a patch of dirt divided by a fence coming out from the middle of the Quonset hut, which ran straight to the street. One of my most significant and even almost inexplicable ministry experiences happened at one of these duplexes.

One Sunday afternoon, my classmate and I walked along different parallel streets, so I was alone. I approached the door on the duplex's right side, looking at it from the perspective of the street. As I approached the door, I heard uproarious laughter coming from inside. The door I was about to knock on was covered with strange markings and colors. After I knocked, I noticed tiny bones and charms on the doorframe, and even a horseshoe, also with markings and splashes of red. My knock was followed by sudden quiet inside. Given the door with its markings and the fact that I was all alone, the sudden quiet unnerved me. I was about to leave in a hurry when the door opened a crack, and a half-face peered through it.

In Afrikaans, I began explaining that I was there to give them a Bible and answer any questions about the Bible they might have. The lady at the door cackled and spoke over her shoulder in her tribal language to whoever was inside, and the howling laughter resumed. She slammed the door. Quite frankly, I was relieved. I think this house was probably one of the many small *shebeens,* which made and sold illegal tribal potions and liquor. I turned and began to walk at an angle toward the end of the center fence to get to the other side of the duplex. I was almost to the end of the fence when I heard the door open and close. A voice spoke in Afrikaans, giving the order which meant, "Sic 'em!" I turned and looked back only to see a terrifying sight. A midsized mangy cur was coming around the corner extremely fast. The picture in my memory is still frighteningly vivid.

The dog was primarily black, with one ear pointed up and the other flopping down. Its tail was trying to stick out behind it, but being broken, it veered off at an angle. The cur was snarling, not barking or wagging its broken tail. He came straight for me, and there was only one thing I could do because running was not an option; there was nowhere to hide. I lifted my briefcase as a flimsy shield and cried out in the Name of the Lord. My background as a missionary kid, raised in the dynamic ministry of my parents, made me aware of the refuge found by calling upon His Name. I cried out in English, "In the Name of Jesus Christ, leave me alone." An extraordinary thing happened next.

Suddenly, a little African boy dressed only in a long white t-shirt had his arms around the neck of the dog, dragging it to the ground. The little boy shouted, "*Hamba! Hamba!*" Meaning, "Get away from here!" I "hamba-ed" very fast! I believe it was the Name of Jesus Christ, in that moment, which brought protection from an angel in the form of a little boy.

I could still see at that age. The dirt lot in front of the Quonset hut was utterly bare. The little boy had been nowhere in sight, and then to suddenly be right there, not running up and yelling at the dog, but right there, with his arms around the neck of the dog, indicated to me that God had sent him. But one more inexplicable element adds to this equation. The word "*hamba*" was not native to the tribes that lived and worked in that area. It was a Zulu word from a completely different part of the country, and it was one of the few words I knew in Zulu, and I knew no words in the local tribal languages. The little boy could not have known that I would have understood that word. Angel or not, I had taken shelter in the Name of the Lord, and the aggressive dog could not attack me.

The Power of the Message of the Gospel

We have discussed how the Holy Spirit, the Cross with the blood, and the Name of the Lord Jesus Christ, by themselves are a mighty arsenal. But the message of the gospel, the Good

News, is a powerful weapon in and of itself. Paul says this in Romans 1:16, "For I am not ashamed of the gospel, for it is the power of God for salvation to everyone who believes...."

Now we know the gospel represents all the theological aspects of salvation, but it also includes all the delightful components of the Good News; these components include peace, forgiveness, freedom, joy, and everlasting life, just to mention a few. The believer's witness about what Jesus has done for them personally is often the most genuine and salient component of the gospel to a not-yet believer. This is because the personal witness of an individual creates applications that the hearer can identify with. A not-yet believer can see hope and joy in a person who, in their estimation, would otherwise be depressed. They can see freedom as a reality in an addict or alcoholic who a controlled substance had enslaved. They can sense peace where there could have been turmoil. On a practical level, the Good News, as seen in a believer's life, is the weapon called the gospel, which is the power of God for salvation.

I met a man, I will call him Roy, in a midsized town in Southern Oregon where we had started a church. He was born and raised in India until coming to the United States as a young man in his twenties. Roy's father was a Hindu priest, but Roy became quite disillusioned with the myths about the Hindu origins of humanity and the world. While in college in India, the mythical legends about different gods and goddesses he had grown up with became ridiculous to him, so he began to look at Catholicism, thinking that the Father, Son, and Spirit, along with Mary, and all the saints, made a more acceptable pantheon of gods. So, despite his family disinheriting him then, he began eagerly integrating into the Catholic religion, which was very strong in his part of India. He loved the stained glass and the incense and the altars and shrines. It was so somber and spiritual to him until he noticed the lack of change inside of himself. He was the same man with the same emptiness of soul as he was as a Hindu.

One day, Roy met two Jehovah's Witnesses (JWs) at his front door. He heard them out and became intrigued with their dedication to their faith. Because he had already made one religious move, the second move was easier to make and came without the familial consequences. He dove into learning their teachings and ways and became a fervent "door-knocker" for the religion. The Indian leadership of the Jehovah's Witnesses saw promise in him and offered to get him into the Watchtower headquarters in New York for further training. The thrill of moving from India to New York, the "Mecca" of the JWs, took less than a year to wear off because, as he told me, the Indian team he'd been a part of back home in India had been much more devout than anyone he had met at the Watchtower Society headquarters in New York. His personal sense of emptiness had become a chasm in his soul.

The day came when he just walked out of the Watchtower Society campus and got on a bus heading west. The details of his next religious adventure are a little fuzzy in my memory, but I remember this much: Somewhere in the Midwest, he was hired to teach in a New Age center. He said this move was not about faith but a job. He called his brand of New Age teaching "Westernized Hinduism for the American Market." He told me he would have stayed there indefinitely because he liked the job perks and the ability to stuff down the emptiness in his soul if it had not been for a severe physical pain in his stomach that made him a mere shadow of himself. Again, the day came when Roy boarded another bus and headed west because he didn't like the part of America he was in. This trip ended when he ran out of money 105 miles inland from the Pacific Ocean.

He now found himself in a town, which happened to be the town in which I was pastoring. He said he needed to "Wait till his money caught up with him," whatever that meant, and then he would move on. By now, the pain in his stomach was almost unbearable. He rented a little room in an old crumbling motel, which had been converted into many one-bedroom apartments. His next-door neighbor, I will call him Dave, was a man with severe epilepsy who had recently received Christ through the witness of a Child Evangelism Fellowship worker from our church, "Grandma Bonnie." Dave would ride his bike to our church about a mile down the road. He asked Roy if he would be willing to meet me, which he was. I first went to Dave's apartment to meet Roy. After our first encounter, I began meeting with Roy in his apartment.

One afternoon, Roy surprised me by walking to my office. Now, here's the good news about the Good News. I seated Roy in the *empty seat* on a couch across from my comfy chair in my office. I already knew much of his story, so I asked him if I could show him something that was not about religion but a relationship with God. I genuinely believe he was there in my office because the Lord had directed him across continents and many miles. Roy was ready for Good News. I pulled out a chart drawn on a poster board I had used in a class. (I will explain that chart in a later chapter.) I put the chart on the floor between us and, using it, explained from 1 Thessalonians 5:23 what it meant to be holy in spirit, soul, and body. He asked many questions, sometimes with excitement, questions about the makeup of a person and the trinity, forgiveness, and faith, and yes, about emptiness in the soul.

Roy slid off the couch onto his knees and scrutinized the chart. After several minutes, he tapped on the chart and said, "I've traveled across the world to see and hear this. I want this. I need this." The truth of the Good News was, at that moment, the power of God for Salvation.

Roy never made it to the Pacific Ocean. He died from cancer eight months later. Before dying, he insisted that he be baptized. Because of his health, I was reluctant to do it until he told me that he could not think of a better way to die than while being baptized. He was so frail and so light that when I laid his head back in the water, his feet came up and popped out of the water. He said, "Brother Harry, I want you to get all of me wet." So, I pushed down on his torso until all of him was under the water. He reemerged out of the water with a huge, bright smile on his dark face. Roy's story is the power of Good News.

An exciting appendix to Roy's story is that, not long after his death, Dave, Roy's neighbor who had invited him to meet me, died in his home with a grand mal seizure. All of this begs the same question I asked before, in a different story: What if Grandma Bonnie hadn't been an ambassador for Christ in Dave's life? And what if Dave hadn't been there and reached out when Roy came to town with an empty soul?

The Power of the Word of God

The power of the Word of God is succinctly stated in Hebrews 4:12-13:

> The Word of God is living and powerful, and sharper than any two-edged sword, piercing even to the division of soul and spirit, and of joints and marrow, and is a discerner of the thoughts and intents of the heart, and there is no creature hidden from His sight, but all things are naked and open to the eyes of Him to whom we must give account. (NKJV)

Jesus said of His own Words in John 8:51, "Most assuredly, I say to you, if anyone keeps my word, he shall never see death." And earlier, in 6:63, "It is the Spirit who gives life; the flesh profits nothing. The words that I speak to you are spirit, and they are life."

Jesus knew His own words were God's power. Remember the Roman centurion who came to Jesus, as seen in Matthew 8:5-13, asking for healing of his faithful servant. This centurion is commended by Jesus for his extraordinary faith because he somehow knew that Jesus' words alone could heal his servant even at a distance. Look at verses 8 and 13.

The centurion answered and said, "Lord, I am not worthy that you should come under my roof. But only speak a word, and my servant will be healed." Then Jesus said to the centurion, "Go your way; and as you have believed, so let it be done for you." And his servant was healed that same hour. (NKJV)

John 1:1 tells us that Jesus is the Word and Jesus is God. In verse 14, John explains that the Word, Jesus, became flesh and lived with us so that humanity could see what God is like. In short, Jesus walking around here on the earth was the Living Word. And His words, while alive on the earth, were the Living Word. And the words inspired by His Spirit through other biblical authors are also His Living Word. We looked at John 6:63, where Jesus said, "It is the Spirit who gives life; the flesh profits nothing. The words that I speak to you are spirit, and they are life" (NKJV). So, *all* of the Word, the Bible, is living and powerful, as the author of Hebrews said. In ministering the gospel, the Word is an extraordinarily powerful weapon, that if we do not wield it, we limit the spread of the gospel by not appropriating His power.

The Gideons, the organization that famously provides Bibles in hotel rooms, share beautiful testimonies of the independent work of the Word of God in people's lives, and they could be well recorded in this chapter here, except that I have chosen to use my own firsthand stories and those of my family and people I know. Countless people's lives have been changed simply through picking up and reading God's powerful Word that they found sitting in that drawer in their hotel room.

In the previous chapter, I wrote about a little girl named Kitty who was delivered from a demon, and the salvation of her father, mother, and her brother, Albert. I want to take you back into that story, to an earlier point, because it tells of the power of the Word. It is not clear in my memory how my dad and Albert met, but somehow an arrangement was made between the two of them to meet at Albert's home, so my dad could tell him from the Bible about Jesus. Albert was a young adult and a diver by trade. As I said before, the Jacobs family was Hindu, and as I have also said before, there are times when Hindus like to learn about other gods to add to their superstitious ways. Many Hindu households have, amongst the shrines to other gods, a picture portraying Jesus.

My dad, however, was not prepared for Mr. Jacobs to grab an *empty seat* and pull it up behind his son as my dad began to show Albert from the Word about Jesus Christ and faith in Him. Dad was not even sure if Mr. Jacobs understood English. This meeting arrangement occurred several times on Albert's day off from work.

One day, my dad knew it was time to invite Albert to respond to the Word he had been learning from about Christ and His atonement. He asked Albert if he wanted to confess Jesus as Lord and to surrender to Him by faith for salvation. Up to this point, Albert had not been inhibited by his dad's presence behind him as he interacted with my dad and the Word. However, on this day, Albert seemed nervous about the question my dad asked of him. He hummed and hawed and moved in his chair, trying to cast a furtive look over his shoulder. Finally, Albert decided, and he told my dad that he very much wanted to become a follower of Jesus. Not knowing what to expect, my dad was shocked to hear Mr. Jacobs, who was still sitting behind his son, speak for the first time. He said in English, "Me too. I believe too; I want to follow too." The Word had penetrated like a sword into Mr. Jacobs' soul because it is powerful on its own.

A similar thing happened with a young man (I will call him Tom) who was attending one of our churches we planted here in America. I started meeting with him one-on-one for discipleship. As part of his discipleship, Tom decided to witness to one of his friends. They were meeting in his friend's kitchen, and the Word was being spoken as Tom shared scripture. Finally, Tom's friend knew that the Jesus that Tom had found was who he needed, too. They prayed together, and his friend accepted Christ as his personal Savior. What Tom did not know was that his friend's wife had been listening from around the corner of the kitchen, and when they finished praying, the man's wife came out with tears in her eyes. She referred to a scripture she had overheard them discussing, and she knew it was what she needed as soon as that scripture had been spoken. Again, the Word pierced this young woman's soul and put light on a need in her inner person.

Jesus' final statements to His closest followers, the men

called disciples, or "learners," were, "Go therefore and make disciples..." (Matthew 28:19). And in Acts 1:8, "...you will be my witnesses...." After being commissioned, His disciples became known as apostles, or "sent ones." The essence of being a disciple-follower of Christ is to go and make more disciple-followers of Jesus Christ. We, too, are learner-followers who become "sent ones." Understanding this, we can freely revel in all the power Jesus has placed behind the presentation of the gospel.

Think about it. The Power of the Spirit of Jesus, the Power of His Cross and blood, the Power of His Name, the Power of the Good News itself, and the Power of His own Word are explosive power! But we are not done yet. The next chapter is devoted entirely to the Power of prayer in the ministry of the gospel of Jesus Christ. It's really something extraordinary to consider.

CHAPTER 5
THE POWER OF PRAYER BEHIND EVANGELISM

I am not a historian, but I like history because it reminds us about essential things we so easily forget. As far as I know, every revival in history, great and small, has come out of strategic prayer. For example, in 1857, New York City had a significant unemployment problem. About thirty thousand men were troubled and hopeless on the streets, with no work and nowhere to go. All of this so moved a businessman named Jeremiah Lamphier that he asked other Christian businessmen to join him in the business district downtown, during lunchtime, to pray with him once a week. During the first lunchtime, on September 23, 1857, six men joined him to pray. After that, the numbers increased each week. Fourteen businessmen came to pray. Then the number increased to twenty-three, and then forty businessmen were praying together! Within weeks, Lamphier's powerhouse of prayer grew to over a thousand who were praying downtown at lunchtime in the business district of New York, and now they were not praying once a week but every day. So began what came to be known as the Folsom Street Revival, and it spread across the entire nation and then around the world. During the next few years, around a million *empty seats* were filled in American churches out of a population of thirty-five million. At one point, it is recorded that there were about ten thousand conversions a week in New York City alone. All this happened because one man began to pray.

The American missions movement came about from a prayer meeting in a field, under a haystack, during an electric storm. Five young men who planned to pray together in a field were caught in a storm, and instead of dispersing, took refuge under sodden hay and supplicated for the crying needs of their world. These five students from Williams College, in Massachusetts, not only started the organizations that funded and sent missionaries around the world, but four of the five young men went overseas themselves.

You may be thinking, "But that was ancient history, way back then. What about now?" America is no longer the world's leading missions sending country. As of the writing of this book, South Korea has eclipsed America as the world's foremost missions sending country on a per capita basis. That should not come as a shock because the explosion of the gospel in that country has come out of churches that have made prayer their primary function. Many of them are having daily prayer meetings that last for hours, not just once a day but both morning and evening. When it comes to prayer, God is no respecter of persons as it relates to their church type, or what their gender is, or what their race or their nationality or country is. He just honors prayer. He honors prayer for souls anywhere.

The question for each one of us is this: Are we talking a good talk about revival, or being a movement, or an un-stoppable force charging the gates of Hell? If we are, but have not backed up our talk with prayer, our words are just rhetoric swirling in the wind with nowhere to land. Prayer is more than just words. Prayer is the act of faith that God will honor. Have you ever thought about the fact that prayer is the only real complete exercise of faith that the believer has on a day-to-day basis? There are other actions that we do because we believe, but they tend to be visual and tangible. With prayer, we cannot see a tangible, visible entity, and our requests are just words. This is not the way a human is wired, so prayer is distinctly an act of faith, and the results are out of our control. This, too, goes against the wiring of human nature.

In Matthew 21:22 Jesus says, "And whatever you ask in prayer, you will receive, if you have faith." You see in this text the act of prayer and then the subsequent faith. That is what we must surrender to, the obedience of faith to pray, and then the faith to leave the answer completely up to God. It is easy to get into the rut where we believe we are not acting in faith unless we can feel the emotional intensity as if sweating drops of blood. Let me reiterate. Faith in prayer is the obedience in taking time to pray for what is close to God's heart and then leaving the burden right there and watching for what God decides to do with our prayer. The power of prayer behind evangelism is not our intensity or our feelings. It is the prayer itself.

So often in our prayers, we give God exact instructions about how to respond to our prayer, but Jesus, speaking to the Father, shows us where the absolute control must be when He said this in Luke 22:42, "...Father, if you are willing, remove this cup from me. Nevertheless, not my will, but yours, be done."

The lack of personal control does not in the least bit diminish the power of prayer. It explains it! If the basis for the power of prayer depended on my pathetic attempts, or yours, to explain to God what we think He should do in any given situation, my world would be a mess, and so would yours. God absolutely hears and answers our prayers, but according to His greater plan, not ours. It is hard, as you know, to surrender to this. We must by faith believe what Jesus said, that whatever we ask in prayer by faith, God will answer in His way, which is, by far, the best way.

Collectively looking at the somewhat sad condition of prayer in much of the American Church today, we can begin with what Jesus said in Mark 11:17, "And he was teaching them and saying to them, 'Is it not written, "My house shall be called a house of prayer for all the nations"? But you have made it a den of robbers.'"

Jesus was specifically talking about the temple there in Jerusalem, but I believe there could be three possible applications for a *house of prayer* in our context today, where we can ask, "Is this a house of prayer or something else?" Both

Peter and Paul use terminology about the universal Church being God's temple. Peter says it this way in I Peter 2:5, "You yourselves like living stones are being built up as a spiritual house, to be a holy priesthood, to offer spiritual sacrifices acceptable to God through Jesus Christ." The global (or even just the American) Church today—is it His house of prayer?

A second application that might also be considered for a house of prayer would be a local church, or as stated in Galatians 6:10, a household of faith. The third of these applications would be what Paul, in 1 Corinthians 3:16 says, "Do you not know that you are God's temple...?" and in 2 Corinthians 6:16, "What agreement has the temple of God with idols, for we are the temple of the living God...." So, the apostle Paul is saying you and I, as individuals, are Christ's temple. The stark question for each of these applications then is this. Are we Christ's house of prayer or something else? Is the American Church a house of prayer today? Is your local church a house of prayer? And then the starkest question of all. Am I, are *you*, as temples of God, where the Spirit of God lives, houses of prayer?

Jeremiah Lamphier, in 1857, saw a need and then prayed and then brought others together to pray for that need. As a result, hundreds of thousands of Americans were saved. If you and I, as temples of God, are individual "houses of prayer for all the nations," it then begins the process of our churches becoming houses of prayer. If our individual churches then become "houses of prayer for all the nations," then the Church in America will become a powerhouse of prayer for all the nations. We could say that in our experience, this is impossible. Yet Jeremiah Lamphier, just one businessman by himself, inviting six other men to pray with him, resulted in nothing short of a miracle. And likewise, the five students huddled under a wet haystack supplicating for the needs of the world resulted in God letting them address those needs far beyond what they could have even imagined. The driving power behind the gospel is still prayer.

It is true that sometimes praying for the lost in general terms can feel impersonal. And, I might add, it can be embarrassing for some Christians to admit they do not even know the names of more than a few unsaved people in their own lives. Their relationships consist mainly of other believers, even though they have folks in and out of their lives who need Christ. But does this mean we should not pray for the lost? The story of Lamphier and the story of the five young men should encourage us. Lamphier did not know the names of the hopeless hordes on his city's streets, and the five students from Williams College could not possibly know the names of the countless millions they were supplicating for. We just need to get started! We need to pray! And we need to stick to it! God will direct His *houses of prayer*.

As a young pastor, I kept myself in shape by running through the small-town neighborhood where we were starting a church. The best route took me by a home on a corner street where two Rottweiler-looking mutts lived. Every time they would hear me passing, they would dash down the long driveway of their home to give chase. Only two times did I end up having an uncomfortable face-off with these territorial beasties. Most of the time, I made it out of their territory before they caught me, but it wasn't very pleasant. One day, rather than letting my irritation grow, I decided to pray for the occupants of that home. I did not know who they were or what their family name was, but for a year and eight months, generally four times per week, I prayed for the people in that home.

Now fast forward. It was Easter Sunday morning, and our church was prayed-up and ready. The hall where our church plant was meeting was beginning to fill up. The *empty seats* now had people sitting in them. Ten minutes into the service, people were standing across the entire back of the hall with some chairs in the side aisles. We were thrilled! We had an awesome service, and quite frankly, the building rocked with energy and joy. At the end of my message, I gave an invitation for salvation. I knew an altar call would be difficult with the hall so crowded, but I asked people to come forward anyway. A few moments into the invitation, two large commercial fishermen standing against the back wall began picking their way down the two side aisles. Both were 6' 8", and it turned out they were brothers. It was a strange and slightly disconcerting sight to behold. I did not know them and wondered if they were coming down for salvation or planned to turn me into a concertina. It turned out that their intentions were salvific. Both brothers and their wives, as well as a teenaged daughter of one of the couples, all made professions of faith that Easter Sunday.

Now for the rest of the story. To my wonderful surprise, I found out they were the family that lived on the corner with the two Rottweilers. I had not known who lived in that home, and I certainly had not known their names to mention in my prayers, but God did. He prompted me to pray, and He drew them to Himself. A funny sidebar to the story: As I ran by their home, they didn't know who I was either, but they admitted they had seen the dogs chasing me and thought it was funny. But it was all worth it! My prayers for this family were unspecific, but God knew their names. We must pray for the lost, whether we know them by name or not.

Jesus would break away from his disciples and the crowds to find a private place to pray. Go figure. Why did Jesus need to pray? Well, I do have some ideas, but it is enough to say that this indeed was His practice right up until just before His crucifixion, while in the garden of Gethsemane, personally doing battle with darkness. Jesus told Peter He had prayed for him while a spiritual battle raged, probably without Peter even knowing about it. In Romans and Hebrews, we are told He prays for us, too.

In addition to Jesus' prayers, we see the early Church depending on prayer. In Acts chapters 1 and 2, we learn that the Church was launched out of the days when one hundred and twenty disciples, both men and women, prayed together. The result happened on Pentecost, where three thousand were saved. In Acts 4:31, we see that the growth of the early Church continued to be driven by the power of prayer, "And when they had prayed, the place in which they were gathered together was shaken, and they were all filled with the Holy Spirit and continued to speak the word of God with boldness."

Acts 2:42 says that the early Church devoted itself to prayer.

In Acts 6:4, men were set apart for time-consuming areas of service so that the apostles could devote themselves to prayer and ministering the Word. In Acts 12, a prayer meeting at John Mark's mother's home prayed Peter out of his chains in prison, so Peter could continue preaching the gospel. It is clear the power behind the gospel has always been prayer, and that will never change. But what has changed is the fact that many of our own churches have forgotten this powerful truth.

For over forty years, God called me to start churches and pastor them, one church-planting opportunity at a time. During this time, I was first legally blind and then started losing more and more of my sight. I was going from seeing some peripheral forms to seeing just shadows. But during the most significant percentage of those years, I had already lost the rest of what little sight I had. I went from being legally blind to totally blind. From a human standpoint, I had virtually nothing going for me. But what I did have was prayer. I have always had prayer, and I will always have prayer. It has been, and always will be, the driving force of anything and everything I am involved with in life and ministry. What an amazing resource we all have once we figure that fact out. Quite frankly, if I am not relying on prayer, I will not be worth anything in ministry. But, as God's children, we all have everything we could possibly need, in that we have access, with freedom, to the throne room of God, and we have the privilege of going to God on behalf of the world around us.

Early in my ministry career, as a pastor and church planter, my family and I had just moved to begin ministering in a town of fewer than 700 people. Because I was the new guy in town, and a pastor at that, I was asked to pray at the beginning of the town's 4th of July picnic. It just so happened that a huge rainstorm was rolling up the Columbia River, and we knew we were in for a deluge. Because we are God's children, we have the right to ask Him for anything, in His Name, so it did not even cross my mind that it would be presumptuous to pray for the rain to bypass our celebration. So, I prayed the opening prayer with the entire crowd hearing my request that God would hold back the rain for their 4th of July picnic. In little time, the folks started commenting that the clouds were separating just before the town and rejoining each other upriver past the town. For the years we were there, I repeatedly heard how that prayer at that event made an impression. It caused people to reconsider church and faith. We are God's children. We can ask, just as long as we remember that God decides. I believed it then, and I believe it now, especially when it comes to the ministry of the gospel.

A few years later, in another small town, there were no resources for the poor and transient community on Highway 101. When we first started a church in that town, we met in a rented hall on Sunday mornings. It was far from ideal, but it served the purpose.

Next door to the hall was a huge building that was amazingly located right on the highway. Every week, when I came to the hall we were renting, I was very moved that the large building next to us would be the best building for a ministry in that town.

One Sunday after church, I walked around the building and prayed about its use for ministry. I began doing this every Sunday, as well as other times during the week, whenever I passed by on foot. Sometimes I circled the building but always stopped to pray. At that time, our church plant was way too small to have any use for it ourselves, but I felt that the building needed to be used in ministry someway somehow.

Let me fast-forward a couple of years, during which time this well-located building went from being a thriving business to being the centerpiece of a lawsuit. It was now sitting empty. I realized that it could be used to serve the tremendous need for a ministry to the poor. Still praying regularly about the building, I contacted the lawyer overseeing the building during the lawsuit. I offered to pay enough rent to cover maintenance, but I told him we could not pay market value as a nonprofit.

Even though he assured me there was no chance of using this facility, I persisted and asked him to ask the owners, who lived out of state, if they would consider our offer. He was chagrined when he got back to me because the owners were willing to rent to us. The lawyer asked me to give him the price we would be willing to pay in order to rent it during the legal settlement time. I gave him a price, trusting God that if He gave us access to the building, we would be able to pay it. My price was just a fraction of what it was worth. But the lawyer agreed, and he even said the owners had that exact amount in mind for covering essential maintenance.

That building, sitting at a critical intersection in town on Highway 101 in Oregon, became the home of a ministry of our church plant. We called it "Abundant Life Ministries," caring for the needs of the poor and destitute locals and transients with food, clothing, groceries, and gas vouchers. We never gave away anything without also offering the gospel, the Good News, as the reason behind the gift. No one ever turned down the opportunity we offered to hear a brief presentation of the gospel. One year, there were one hundred and four professions of faith in that ministry, all funded by our thrift store and our bookstore in that miracle building. God honors prayer, and faith, and outreach to the lost, rich or poor. It is all proof of the power of prayer.

As a blind or partially blind pastor, I have prayed for safe passage across highways where there was no possible way for me to cross safely. I have asked God to get me to addresses I could not see while doing visitation on foot. I have prayed and trusted God to help me remember scriptures and content in messages because I could not see to use notes.

I have had to, in more recent years, pray for His divine guidance while flying, like boarding shuttle busses, changing gates in airports, getting in the right line for the right desk, and even finding restrooms. I tell you this because praying and trusting God while in ministry or any other walk of life is real life, and I can say to you He has never failed me yet. God delights in us when we ask and believe, and then we get on with it.

One of the fears about prayer is letting others know what we are praying for. We often use the excuse we think it would be prideful to tell others, but God can handle His reputation.

We fear what we prayed for will not happen, but if God leads, pray. Let Him worry about His results.

Remember Elijah on Mount Carmel in First Kings 18? There was no doubt about the prayer challenge with the priests of Baal. If God had not come through for Elijah, he would have been slaughtered. My own experiences with events approximating prayer challenges have left me as a full believer in what God will do for the cause of the gospel and His Glory.

One of these experiences happened during a difficult time in our family. I was between my first church plant and my next pastorate, which was not a church plant. We had an incredible ministry in planting that first church, but I made a stupid, prideful, rookie mistake. I left the church too early. After doing so, I believe God let me take our family through a difficult time to help me learn from my stupidity.

During this time, God was still very much present in our lives. I'm telling you this because we must remember that God knows what is needed to keep us focused on His plan and purpose in our individual lives and our ministry. He still wanted to use us for His glory, but I needed a course from His school of hard knocks.

To feed my family, I went to work for a contractor who installed septic tanks (God does have a sense of humor). He teamed me up with a man who happened to be a Jehovah's Witness Elder. We, of course, had many great conversations about faith. One day, after it had rained hard for days, and the construction site, which sat on a steep hill, was a muddy, slippery mess, the Kingdom Hall Elder, Dick, and I arrived for work.

We were in a 4x4 pickup, and it threw mud everywhere, but it still could not find traction to go up the hill and slid back down instead. He slammed the truck into extra-low four-wheel drive and took another run at it with no success. He was about to turn around and leave when I proposed the prayer challenge. He smirked at me and said, "That's stupid," but not wanting to miss a challenge, he said he would try again, anyway.

Dick backed up as far as he could, and then he paused deliberately for a moment, a moment in which I believed he was stopping to pray to his god before he took the next run at the hill. All four tires were spinning hard, with mud flying everywhere. The engine screamed as the tires struggled to grip the dirt under the muddy surface. But alas, we slid back down. He mumbled an expletive under his breath and started turning the truck around. I put my hand on his hand as he went to switch gears.

I said, "Dick, fair is fair. It's my turn to pray. I'm going to pray, and then let's take one more try at the hill." I am sure he only cooperated because, at this point in his mind, it was a hopeless cause. I prayed out loud for God to show Himself to Dick. After I prayed, Dick put the truck into gear and— wait for it— yes, it walked right up the hill. He grumbled to me, "That means nothing. The top mud was thrown off by our earlier attempts. That's all."

For the rest of the day, he was unusually quiet. In my heart, I knew God had shown Himself to Dick. But a strange and somewhat disappointing thing happened. Dick never came back to work. When I enquired about him, I was told he had suddenly left town without a forwarding address. His *seat* behind the wheel of that 4x4 truck ended up *empty*.

Let me say this. Things that happen while fishing for souls do not always work out the way we think they should. I still pray for Dick to this day, and I know God will continue to show Himself to Dick. God is not willing that any should perish.

Whether as individuals or church based, if our motives are right and we feel led by God to take a prayer stand, we must do it. The results are God's problem. God knows what He is doing. When we pray, we are God's house of prayer for the nations, as individuals, as local churches, and as the Church around the world. And this raises a question in my mind. What movement of God or revival is not happening today because Christians use the rhetoric, but do not supplicate, which is the actual act of faith? The power behind evangelism must include prayer, the Living Word, the Good News itself, the almighty Name of Jesus, the power of His blood, and of course, the Spirit of Jesus upon us, in us, and for us, in our ministry.

CHAPTER 6
LIFE MESSAGE

Think about the term used for this chapter title. *Life message.* The message of your life and my life in its entirety. As you sit where you are, reading this book at this moment, you are a compilation of your experiences to date, with your body and your mind, your emotions and your intelligences, your education along with other learning, and your temperament, and do not forget your spiritual gift. Would God not be wasting a lot if He only used your spiritual giftedness? Well, the truth is, He does not want to waste any of it. Your life message includes all the above and then some. You and I are unique instruments for service in the hands of the Holy Spirit. We are not duplicates or in any way redundant. Each of us is designed individually to be used for serving Christ, whether in the household of faith or in reaching those on the outside.

A craftsman, a dentist, a surgeon all operate using distinct tools for specific functions. The same is true for the Master Craftsman, our Maker. When He creates us as new creatures, He makes us distinctly different and uniquely usable. We are dynamic tools in Christ's work of reconciling the world to Himself. 2 Corinthians 5:17-20 shows that this work of reconciliation of the Master is done by using us, His fully gifted people, as the instruments of reconciliation. Let me offer some biblical examples of individuals, each with his or her unique life message, being used as unique tools of the Master Craftsman.

In 1 Corinthians 3 and 4, the apostle Paul speaks to the Corinthian church of himself in such a way that we catch a glimpse of his life message. In 3:6, he identifies his ministry as a planter. In 3:10, he identifies as being an architect. In 4:15-16, he identifies as a father to be imitated. He gives these glimpses of himself in juxtaposition to Peter and Apollos because the Corinthian church was getting into comparisons between the three of them. He wanted to explain how each of them had his own function in the Master's hand. With these three descriptions – planter, architect, and father - he indicates that with all that he is, and all that he has been through, he is a starter of ministry and that others with their individual life message come in after him to build on what he has started. This is certainly what we see of him in Acts, from chapter 13 through the end of the book. We see him starting churches all the way to Rome. So, we can see that Paul is a "sent one" (Apostle) for beginning ministry.

As we look at other Bible characters, we see, in retrospect, that they are identified by what we can call their *life message*. For example, Noah built an ark. Abraham believed God and went. Sarah, as an old lady, conceived a promised child. Moses led the tribes of Israel to become the nation of Israel. Joshua conquered Palestine. David was the great king. Mary was the mother of Jesus. John the Baptist was a voice in the wilderness. Stephen was the martyr. And the list goes on. Each of these people had much more to their everyday lives, but they are known by God in His Word as unique operatives in the Master's hand, accomplishing His purpose with the sum total of their lives. This is not in any way to diminish them as people but to point out how every part of each one's life contributed to what the Master Craftsman designed them for.

Are you able to see that Moses's upbringing, as a part of the Egyptian dynasty, clearly gave him needed insight for leading the tribes of Israel out of that land and turning them into a nation? His forty years in the desert leading sheep indeed became a part of leading Israel through forty years in mostly the same desert. Yet, as we know, his huge spiritual function was to be the vessel to receive the Law and bring Israel to live under it.

We can also see how Mary's life and history and genetics contributed to God's calling for her to be the mother of the Messiah. It is not insignificant that she was a virgin, a Jewess, a direct descendent of King David, and fertile for producing a child, the Holy Child, through the work of the Holy Spirit. Additionally, she was raised as a spiritually faithful Israelite in a Jewish community and betrothed to a man who was exactly right for being the dad of her Son. Joseph was also a direct descendant of King David. Once again, we can see how all of this was a part of her great spiritual calling to raise Jesus all the way up to His ministry age.

In the same vein, we spoke earlier about the product of Paul's life as a starter of ministry, but he too was able to function in that role because God used all of who he was. He was a pure-blooded Jew and a Roman citizen. He was educated in Greek culture and the highest levels of Judaism. He had migrated from Tarsus, so he was used to the type of travel he would have to do in ministry. He spoke at least three languages, all essential to his calling. Even his violent, forceful approach before his salvation, as Saul, when he was propagating Jewish beliefs, made his conversion, and his now passionate fervent approach, a thing of significance to many in Judah and elsewhere in the world. This backstory was useful for the Holy Spirit to reach through Paul's spiritual giftedness, designed by the Master Craftsman for His function and to His glory.

All of these are illustrations of what I'm calling a *life message*, and here's the beautiful thing: Each of us also has a fully functional message of our own lives, in its entirety, a life message which is custom made for unique usability to function in the hand of the Master Craftsman. In Ephesians 2:10, Paul says that we are God's *work of art*. The word in the English text is usually "workmanship," but in Greek, the word is "Poiema," which gives us our English words "poem" and "poetry." To me, this makes it easier to extrapolate further about its meaning. I like to say, that as God's poem, He uses our unique rhythm and rhyme, or the way we roll, to reach the world. Remember, as I said before, we are now the flesh-and-blood body of Christ in our world. The Master Craftsman knows exactly what our life message is designed for, and it can give each of us great peace to understand what our usability is and what it is not.

As a twenty-four-year-old, God started teaching me this concept through His Word, and I must tell you, I have relished watching it develop in my life for all these years in ministry. Realizing that I, Harry Olsen, have a life message and then beginning to see a glimpse of what my life message is, has helped me fine-tune my usefulness in the Master's hand. My wife Carol and I, along with our six-month-old little girl, joined up with another couple to run small local evangelistic crusades and Bible conferences from Bellingham, Washington, to San Diego, California. The five of us were traveling in a Volkswagen van, passing by Mount Shasta in northern California. We stopped at a viewpoint on Interstate-5 to gaze at Black Butte and see Mount Shasta towering over it. Right there, while leaning on the front of the van, I prayed a prayer that would prove to be a seminal moment in my life and ministry career. I asked God to give me a glimpse of the epitaph that He would like to write about my life when my life was done on this earth. This is not as ghoulish a request as it might sound.

That morning, I had read Acts 13:36, where Paul was preaching, and he said this about King David, that David "...had served the purpose of God in his generation...." After reading this, I thought at the time that this sounded like a good epitaph. I even tried it out by saying, "Here lies Harry Olsen. He served God's purpose in his generation." Musing further, it

came to me that it would be great to identify a personal
purpose or message of my life as a compass or a beacon on a
hill, which could be consulted for direction throughout my life.
So that day, leaning on the front of that VW Van, I found
myself praying that prayer, asking God if He would give me a
glimpse of what He would like to write as a summary of my life.

For about three weeks, I prayed that prayer daily. Then one
morning, while reading my Bible, there it was staring at me, and
my heart knew it was the answer. It was the essence of my
epitaph, and for more than forty years, that epitaph has become
a focus for the development of the message of my life. It is a
beacon on a hill, a compass. It allows all of me and the experiences that God has taken me through to be used in my world.
When I am praying and thinking about a huge choice or decision, I measure the possibilities against that life message that
God clarified for me through that verse. When I become aware
of an opportunity to represent the claims of Christ in some part
of my context, I look for opportunities to have those claims
flow through who I am, not through planned approaches or
memorized words.

In 1 Thessalonians 5:23, Paul is praying, and he identifies the
components of a person being spirit, soul, and body. In this
chapter, I include a simple chart, which comes out of this verse.
I have used this chart for evangelism, discipleship, and even
counseling. For now, let me use it to help all of us understand
that each of us has a life message. Don't get me wrong. The
trichotomous picture shown in this verse is not the only break-
down of a person that we see in the scriptures, but it is one of

them, and it is the one I like to use because it is very user-friendly.

We all recognize that while alive on Earth, a person has a *body*. Most Bible studies and teachers also acknowledge the existence of the eternal *soul* from conception. But let me bring to the discussion some biblical teachings about *spirit*.

Genesis 1:26 says, "Then God said, 'Let us make man in Our image, after Our likeness.'" In response, we must ask this question: What is God's likeness and image? John the apostle, in his Gospel, verse 4:24, quotes Jesus as saying, "God is Spirit." Pulling this together then, we see God has put spirit in every person, which some would call a God-shaped vacuum or a place for Himself. I have human spirit, as do you, and when salvation takes place, God seals us with His Holy Spirit in our spirit, taking occupancy forever with what is called Everlasting Life (Ephesians 1:13-14). This means then, at this moment, because I have received Jesus Christ as my personal Savior, I, Harry, have a body, I have a soul, and I have a spirit that is my human spirit, now fully occupied by the divine Spirit, the Spirit of Jesus Christ.

This is also wholly true of you as a child of God. I am not sure how this truth makes you feel, but personally, knowing God's Spirit is in me gives me incredible stature in my world. I am a different kind of humanoid, one that is not only a human person but also one that has the Spirit of the Divine in me for the rest of my life. 2 Corinthians 5:17, which I referenced earlier, clearly states this. When I became a Christian, I became a new kind of creation. Wow! That makes me want to stand up and shout, "Hallelujah!"

Now, let's bring all of this into the wonders of our unique life message, which is a compilation of everything in each of us. Everything that is the personal history of our body, and every-thing true—past and present—of our soul, become engaged by God's Spirit in our human spirit to be a unique brush stroke of His spiritual giftedness in each of us. God's holy giftedness reaches through everything uniquely me, and through every-thing uniquely you, to reach our worlds for His cause of salva-tion because He is not willing that any should perish.

Our bodies include our appearance, our age, our sex, our race, our physical prowess or limitations, our genetic ties to other human beings, our athletic ability, to name just a few of the prominent characteristics. Beyond our bodies, we are designed with the human soul. My understanding is that soul includes our emotional structure, mental capacity, and volition or will to make things happen from out of emotions and mind. Then we add to what we just talked about, our spirit. As born-again Christians, the Spirit of Jesus Christ has become one with our individual spirits, coupled with our physical body and soul, thus creating in each of us a supernatural ability for service that is commonly called a spiritual gift. I will be going into much more detail regarding spiritual gifts, as they relate to soul winning, in the next chapter. For now, let me expand a little further on life's message.

There are specialists on brain function and the operation of the mind who tell us our physical action becomes empowered by what is inside of us. They say this is partially accomplished by each person having between seven and eleven intelligences that give our minds and bodies skills. Each of us, as I understand it, have all these aforementioned intelligences, but in differing orders. Along with this, the unique structure of each of our temperaments, plus the opportunities in our lives, give our volition the direction that drives every person to their actions. So, bundling the way our minds and emotions work, together with our experiences and our physical assets, the Master Craftsman has designed in us total and absolute uniqueness. He then reaches through this uniqueness with an individualized spiritual gift so that He, the Spirit of God, can minister to our worlds in hundreds of specialized ways. I believe that God has chosen to work this way in saving souls. All of this is

what I have been calling a life message. Simply put, the message
of our lives is useable for the gospel. God knows this message
well, and it is what He uses when He places us in the circumstances to serve. Because I am very aware of all this, when I
pray for the occupant of the *empty seat* next to me on a flight, I
fully expect that God in His wisdom will send a person to sit in
that seat who has a need that my life's message can minister to.

A few years ago, on a flight from Seattle to Denver, I had
been seated by the attendant in the seat I think of as the
obstacle seat. On a 737, that is the seat right up front that
everyone boarding must go around, and with my 6'1" frame in
it, I have to pull my shoulders together and tuck my legs way
back until the plane is completely boarded, and then I have to
watch my feet for the entire trip. I do not like to sit there
because I am an inconvenience. But in retrospect, on this flight
I thank the Lord for this spot and the seat next to it. No one
filled the *empty seat* until just before they closed the door.

As the attendant closed the door, I heard a voice saying,
"Hello! Hello! Wait! Wait!" The attendant held the door and
invited an out-of-breath lady to board. With an apology, she
explained she had gone to the wrong gate, which made her late.
She was excited to see an *empty seat* next to me and asked if it
was still open. I said it was and welcomed her. After the flight
attendant found space in the overhead racks for the lady's bags,
and after all the flight instructions were given, which we could
not possibly ignore as the flight attendants doing the demon-
strations were almost on top of us, the jet taxied down the
runway and leaped into the air.

By divine appointment, the *empty seat* next to me was now occupied by the person God had designed to sit there. Her name was Carla. He already knew Carla needed what the Holy Spirit, in and through my life, had planned for her soul and well-being. A few minutes airborne was all it took before Carla said, "You're blind, aren't you?" She went on to say that she had seen me in the concourse and wondered what it was like traveling as a blind person. "So, what's it like?" she asked. I answered, and she followed up with a question about how I became blind and if being blind made me feel bad. I got a thorough interview about not having sight. Carla seemed to need to talk and be verbally engaged without giving me any real opportunity to respond. Her next line of questioning was about the cross I wore. Was I religious? Did I go to church? Was I a priest of some kind? Did I have a church that I pastored? Was I a counselor? And so on.

During this entire time, I had been doing my normal practice of what I call bifurcated listening, a method I use at times like this. It is a practice where I listen with my ears to the person I am desiring to minister to, while inwardly, I am consciously in prayer and listening for a word from God in my spirit. I finally stopped Carla and asked her what was up in *her* life. I told her it was obvious to me she was hurting, and I asked her if she wanted to talk about it. I was not ready for the flood of tears. She wept quietly for a little while, then through her tears, Carla said, "Tomorrow will be ten years."

My seatmate began to tell how her only child was brutally murdered by a predator and buried in a shallow grave in the

countryside; she was only ten. This is what Carla was referring
to when she said, "Tomorrow will be ten years." It would be the
tenth anniversary of her daughter's murder. Because of that
tragedy in her life, for most of the ten years since her daughter's
death, Carla had been off the deep end with drugs and alcohol,
after which she had clawed her way out of addiction through
Alcoholics and Narcotics Anonymous meetings. She'd been
clean and sober for eighteen months. In recent weeks, Carla
had been with family in the Seattle area, dreading the
impending anniversary of her daughter's death. She hoped she
would be okay by being with family, well away from the site
where her daughter had died. As this dear mother got closer to
the date, Carla knew in her heart she could not be out of town.
She felt it would dishonor her little girl. So here she was,
headed toward Denver and terrified of the anniversary, and her
addiction, and life itself.

Without giving our whole dialogue of she said/I said, let me
just say that during that two hour and 35-minute flight, this
hurting lady met the Savior of her soul. And that's exactly what
He did. Jesus saved Carla's soul! She was hoping she had enough
faith to believe for salvation. I showed her Ephesians 2:8-9,
where God promises He would give her the gift of faith
through His grace. When it was obvious to her, she truly understood. I led Carla in a prayer of surrender. What happened next
was something I did not expect. At the end of her prayer, I said
"Amen," and she followed with an "Amen." Then the man to the
left of her in our row said "Amen," and then the man behind
him, who sat in the next row by the window, said "Amen," too!

To top off this unusual moment, the flight attendant, who had spent quite a bit of time standing and leaning against the bulkhead in front of us, pulled away from the bulkhead and started walking down the aisle. As she passed by me, she warmly tapped me on the shoulder three times, giving my shoulder a little squeeze. What a strange little camp meeting those of us in the front of this 737 had just shared.

Now here is the life message application of this story. The Lord knew I was an older white-haired man and not at all threatening to a woman, probably right around forty years old. Carla had seen me in the concourse as a blind man, and when she sat down, she reached out to someone who probably, she felt, would have empathy because life had, in all likelihood, been tough for me too. She explained to me, after seeing the cross around my neck, that the alcohol and drug addiction meetings she had attended were in church buildings, and she had met some friendly, unthreatening people in those places. Because of that, when Carla found out that I was a pastor, she was not threatened but thrilled. She did not know that I had led drug and alcohol recovery groups for many years, evening teaching in a recovery facility. She did not know I had counseled for many, many hours as a pastor. And she certainly did not know I was ready and prepared for her because I had prayed for the *empty seat* next to me, and God divinely placed her in that *empty seat.*

God works these things out like this: wherever a willing witness is, in this case, me sitting in that obstacle seat on a 737, His Spirit will reach through all of what is that person's life, and

He will use the spiritual gift He has given that person, to lead a lost and hurting soul towards a forever relationship with the Savior of their soul. He is the one and only Person who can save them. That is the absolute beauty of the message of one's life when surrendered to the skillful hand of the Master Craftsman.

The chart, with three circles, probably does not look much like you or me (although some of us are rounder than we should be). But it represents the raw materials that comprise the pallet of colors, out of which the Master Artist works to paint the portrait of your life or the portrait of my life. He is still creating the work of art that is your life message. Yours is beautifully you, and mine is beautifully me, only with the touch of the Master's hand. In theory, there may be some individuals that only you will be able to reach because of the uniqueness of the message of your life.

CHAPTER 7
NO SPIRITUAL GIFT OF EVANGELISM

One of my friends in ministry knows that when it comes to soul winning, I see some doctrinal points a little differently than most. Instead of calling these differences "heresies," he calls my differences by my first name, "Harry-sees." In this chapter, I am going to lay out a couple of "Harry-sees" that will be different than what most people believe and show you how I believe they make a big difference in soul winning. The truth is, neither of these is earth-shattering disclosures that will change the world as we know it, and these points are not about the nature or character of God; they are simply different interpretations of the biblical text. I believe, however, they can free a believer from fears and discomfort in sharing the gospel. These perspectives on evangelism also go well with the understanding from the previous chapter that each believer has a life message.

The first of these "Harry-sees" is that I believe there is no *separate* spiritual gift of Evangelism, but that *every* spiritual gift is the gift of Evangelism in and of itself. Let me give you an illustration. My wife Carol has the spiritual gift of mercy that has been made clear in many ways in her life. She is now a retired registered nurse, but at the time of this story, she worked in the field of Home Health and Hospice. One of her patients was in the final stage of life, and the family chose to have him hospitalized for his end-of-life care. This man had been a college professor but now was too weak to talk. The first time Carol cared for him, she could tell his life was rapidly slipping away, yet he was still somewhat alert. And Carol noticed something else. There was fear in his eyes. Soon after, Carol went back into his hospital room. At the time, there were no family or friends in the room with him. She had such a strong burden in her soul for him. He was about to face eternity, and she wondered if he was ready.

As is often the case, staff were not really allowed to speak to patients about specific religious beliefs. Hospice patients could choose to speak with a chaplain for comfort, but rarely did the issue of their eternal soul come up, especially in a secular hospital. Knowing this, Carol asked God for grace. She strongly felt that even though she would be breaking the rules, she had to take what might be this man's last opportunity to hear the gospel. She entered the room, which was deathly quiet, and shut the door behind her. Then she quietly asked the Lord specifically to keep the frequent visits of hospital staff at bay, allowing her to have a few uninterrupted moments with him. She sat on the side of his bed.

His eyes followed Carol's every movement. She took his hand in hers and spoke his name. His eyes were engaged with hers. The mercy of God that drives her spiritual gift laid out a simple explanation of the gospel, with an invitation to pray along with her. When she prayed this prayer, he closed his eyes. When she completed the prayer with him, he opened his eyes and looked at her, and ever so slightly, squeezed her hand. Immediately following that mercy moment, she released his hand and stood up, at which point the door opened, and hospital staff began coming and going again.

Carol knew beyond a shadow of a doubt that God had been there in that room, in that moment, and that God had given them those quiet, uninterrupted minutes together. God gave that patient the same chance He gave the thief on the cross next to Jesus. He gave him the opportunity for a last-minute decision to surrender to the Savior's love. Carol knew in her soul this man's eternal destiny was now settled. Carol never had a chance to visit with him again because a day or so later, his life on Earth ended. The truth of this story is that man's new life in the presence of Jesus was only beginning. God had reached through her gift of mercy to offer that ex-college professor salvation one more time.

On another occasion, God used Carol's gift of mercy in another life. Because of the nature of our ministry during this period in our lives, we traveled quite a bit over a four-state region. At the time of this story, we were living in a fifth wheel, and we were parked in an RV park in Sandy, Utah. While there, Carol saw a desolate-looking young lady sitting alone at a picnic table. Carol's gift of mercy sent her to sit at the table and engage the lady. She was Korean and only gave us her initials—KM. She told Carol that her husband, while in a rage, hooked up their house trailer to their truck and proceeded to pull out of the RV Park, leaving her behind with nothing. All she had in the world was in that house trailer. She had no money, no phone, no clothes except what was on her back, and no food.

Carol could see that this young lady had also been slapped around. When Carol sat down on the picnic bench with KM, it was obvious she was all cried out, having puffy red eyes. As it turned out, she had been sitting there for hours. Carol took her into our fifth wheel home and fed her and cared for her, and let her pour out her heart. The man KM called her husband turned out not to be her husband, but an older man who was using her. He never came back. She was with us for two nights, sleeping on our couch until we were able to connect her with a safe Christian place where she could stay and where they would help her figure out the next steps in her life. There is a song called "Mercy Came Running." And in that instance, from the beginning of the first encounter with KM till the end of our time with her, the mercy of God, through Carol, resulted in KM calling on the name of the Lord to be saved. In retrospect, we do not doubt what happened in KM during those days. It was clear that this young lady had gone from *lost* to *hope*. The hope that only God could have given her.

Over these many years, Carol has found that her opportunities for evangelism flow out of the spiritual gift God has given her. These are just two examples of her using her spiritual gift of mercy to become the gift of evangelism for both a dying patient and an abandoned stranger. Whenever and wherever God has led Carol into a personal evangelistic effort, it has always included an act of mercy.

Observing this kind of soul winning that I have been talking about on these pages (soul winning where God reaches through the life message of a person and using that person's spiritual gift, He reaches a soul for Christ) is just one of the reasons I believe there is no separate spiritual gift of evangelism. There is, however, another reason why I believe our spiritual gift *is* the actual gift of evangelism. The reason is that there is never a specific listing in the Bible that says evangelism is a spiritual gift. Take, for example, where the word evangelism is used in Ephesians 4:11-13. It is mentioned alongside other functions of ministry operatives. Let me show you the passage:

And he gave the apostles, the prophets, the evangelists, the shepherds and teachers, to equip the saints for the work of ministry, for building up the body of Christ, until we all attain to the unity of the faith and of the knowledge of the Son of God, to mature manhood, to the measure of the stature of the fullness of Christ.

According to the text, the five types of ministry operatives spoken of in Ephesians are for building up and equipping the body of believers. Two of them are not seen in any spiritual gift lists, one being "evangelists" and the other being "shepherds," or in other translations, "pastors." Both are essential for a local church as ministers or operatives, but neither are listed anywhere as spiritual gifts.

In a similar type of context, we see in Acts 21:8 that Philip is called an evangelist, not as a spiritual gift, but as a minister or operative. In that same vein, in Paul's second letter to Timothy (4:5), he's talking to Timothy about doing all the facets of the pastoral ministry. This is what Paul said, "But you be watchful in all things, endure afflictions, do the work of an evangelist, fulfill your ministry" (NKJV). Once again, Paul isn't talking about a spiritual gift. Paul is telling Timothy to do the *job* of an evangelist. These are the only three references to the word "evangelist" in the New Testament.

Still not convinced? Let me approach this from a different angle, that of a strange omission. Paul, in 1 Timothy 1:5, unequivocally states why God sent Jesus to Earth.

"The saying is trustworthy and deserving of full acceptance that Christ Jesus came into the world to save sinners."

In an earlier chapter, I pointed out what Jesus said of Himself, that He came "… to seek and to save the lost" (Luke 19:10). If Jesus' own mandate when He was in His earthly body was what we call evangelism, it seems strange that, when gifting the church, which is His now-body, His own Holy Spirit would forget to make room for a gift for winning the lost? I'm speaking specifically of the actual lists of spiritual gifts in 1 Corinthians 12, Romans 12, and 1 Peter 4.

Continuing with this line of thought of the priority of Jesus' life, let us ask ourselves if it would be biblically realistic for the Godhead to only place one spiritual gift for the saving of souls. In that perspective, this one gift would be the *only* spiritual gift, out of the list of twenty or more in 1 Corinthians and Romans, for fulfilling what was Christ's very purpose for coming to this earth, to seek and to save the lost. This one gift would be sparsely distributed in His now-body to individuals to do the work of evangelism. In contrast, the rest of the individuals in the body would each be given one of the other gifts from the list, not for seeking and saving the lost but for the specific internal uses in the body of Christ. I say a resounding no! God is not willing that any should perish, so I believe He has gifted the Church accordingly. I cannot believe that of the Savior, given His self-proclaimed mandate for the meaning of His life and His subsequent commissioning of His now-body as stated in Matthew 28:18-20.

I fear, however, some teachers teach this concept of evangelism as one of the specific spiritual gifts because it offers an excuse for not having to be personally accountable for soul winning. On the other hand, I believe that most folks who have accepted this teaching, that evangelism is one of the spiritual gifts, is because they have not personally done their own examination of the texts. It is easy for any of us to receive instruction from others with the assumption that appropriate research has been done. However, without personal study, an individual would have no way of knowing that there may be a better understanding of evangelism. Many, many times, I have heard people say something to this effect: "I feel bad about lost souls, but evangelism is just not my spiritual gift." This, unfortunately, leads to them let themselves off the hook for accountability to reach out to lost souls.

Here again, is my hypothesis. I believe that evangelism is a function of all individuals within the body of Christ as each learns to apply their gift both inwardly and outwardly, serving Christ's kingdom. In this understanding, every gift will be used, in its own way, to reach the lost for whom Jesus died. I intend to show you that, in reality, every spiritual gift is, in and of itself, a form of evangelism. Wouldn't that make more biblical sense?

Let me explain further by adding one more biblical principle that's different from many perspectives regarding spiritual gifts. Still, it works together with what I have been saying up to this point. Please stay with me as I develop this additional concept. It could be exciting and liberating for you. It has been so for me and my wife Carol and for a growing number of others I have shared this point with over the years.

This other concept, or as my friend would say, "Harry-see," is this: I believe every Christian has only *one* spiritual gift. This may, however, have been different for the Twelve Apostles. I am not sure about them. But for the believers of the Church Age, which is you and me, I believe that we each have only *one* spiritual gift. I believe that the specific gift given is used in multiple ways by the Giver of gifts, reaching through our life message. And I believe that the scripture seems to say this specifically. Let's look at Paul's wording in 1 Corinthians 12:8-10. He begins in verse 8 by saying, "For to one is given the word of wisdom through the Spirit, and to another the word of knowledge through the same spirit, to another faith by the same Spirit..." (NKJV). Paul continues through verse 10 using the singular phrase "to another" five more times. Nine gifts are listed in this way as singular stand-alone gifts.

Later in this same chapter, something similar is stated, beginning at verse 28, where Paul uses the numbers one, two, and three as he lists the spiritual gifts again, but for a slightly different purpose. People debate whether this numeric listing is in order of importance or in order of occurrence. The point I am making here is that the gifts are singled out one at a time and not in clusters, once again likely indicating there is only one gift given. The same type of singular wording is true in the other listing of gifts, too. In Romans 12, the expressions are also singular. In the New Living Translation, verses 7 and 8 are stated this way, "If your gift is serving others, serve them well. If you are a teacher, teach well. If your gift is to encourage others, be encouraging...." And so on. In the New King James Version, the same passage is worded this way, "... he who teaches in teaching, he who exhorts, in exhortation; he who gives, with liberality...."

Here is one last scriptural implication regarding this "Harry-see" —one spiritual gift per believer. In 1 Corinthians 12:14-26, Paul makes his point by identifying individual gifts as being individual parts of a body. He uses the foot, the hand, the ear, the eye, and the head. These verses, in juxtaposition with the earlier points, in my perspective, are pretty conclusive. Each believer has one gift that God can use in multiple ways.

Now, let's take what I believe and put it together: there is no separate gift of evangelism, and God can use *every* gift as its own gift of evangelism. Then, let's put that understanding with what I understand about each of us having *one* powerfully focused spiritual gift instead of a cluster of gifts that leave a person trying to order their ministry priorities. Our spiritual gift then becomes fully manifested as our gift of evangelism. The result is that I have a singular, unique, targeted message from my life, especially when we bring in the truths from the previous chapter about all that is our life message.

That each of us has only one gift is not a game-changer for those who teach a mix of gifts. The point I am making here is not entirely nullified if someone believes in a gift mix. Most teachers of the gift mix approach to spiritual gifts will tell you that if you have a mix, you have a primary or lead gift. Putting this gift mix idea to the test, let's look again at the example of my wife. Through Carol's gift of mercy, both the dying college professor and KM were led to a relationship with Christ. If you believe in a gift mix, then the same truth applies. Carol's lead gift of mercy would have been her gift of evangelism in those salvific moments. The concept of a gift mix does not make incompatible the truth that a spiritual gift is used both internally within the body of Christ and externally as outreach in evangelism.

About a year before my dad went home to be with his Lord and Savior, he and I took a walk on Harris Beach in Southern Oregon. I asked him what he thought his spiritual gift was. His answer baffled me. In my estimation, he was the most well-defined Christian worker I had ever known. So, when he told me he wasn't sure, I laughed out loud. I thought he was pulling my leg, but he wasn't. He asked me what I thought it was, and I explained why I thought he had the gift of exhortation. His response was, "You might be right. I really haven't given it much thought." As you can tell by now, I am different from my dad in this way. I have given this subject much thought over the years.

If I was correct about my dad's spiritual gift, this is how I will apply the points discussed in the above paragraphs. In the area of discipleship, his gift became clear to me when I saw his highly defined method resulting in converts who really wanted to do well in Christ as they grew in their faith over time. It was my dad's spiritual gift lifting each of them up to long term possibilities and a lifetime of following Jesus. Anyone who disciples a new believer will know this progressive growth in Christ is not always the end result. His gift was also apparent in church planting by observing the high energy and full expectations of God's miraculous power in the lives of the people in those churches that he planted. As an overseer of church plants, I can personally assure you, that is not always the case. When my dad preached, whether in Africa or here in the states, his gift of exhortation lifted people up to possibilities, as this particular gift always does. His spiritual gift of exhortation would manifest itself repeatedly when he led people, primarily men, to know Jesus as their Savior. These men who had received Christ as Savior through my dad's ministry, many of whom I personally knew, seemed not just to receive Christ but to *embrace* Christ by getting a glimpse of what they could be in relationship with Him. I wish this were always the result for all of us involved in soul winning, but it is not.

The way I see it, my dad had one spiritual gift, which seemed to be the gift of exhortation. With that gift, an individual comes alongside and helps people take the next steps in their faith journey and makes them feel good about doing so. God, the Holy Spirit, skillfully reached through who my dad was, along with his spiritual gift, making my dad useable and suitable in different ways. Whether soul winning, or discipling, or preaching, the effect appeared to be the same. I never saw my dad trying to be someone he wasn't. He knew who God made him to be, and that is who he was. Can you see how liberating this concept could be for you and me? God just wants us to be what He has gifted us to be.

We must not spend time comparing ourselves with other Christians and feeling guilty we have not done what they have. Major soul winning angst revolves around this point because we feel guilt or feel less spiritual when we see or hear of someone else leading a person to Christ. We experience this angst instead of rejoicing with them and then moving on while looking for our own opportunities for soul winning that fit our own life messages and spiritual giftedness. Some life message/spiritual gift combinations will indeed have more opportunities to see tangible final decisions to follow Christ. But do not forget. Their opportunities are built on the witness of other life messages and spiritual gifts, those of individuals who planted seeds at earlier points along the way in a person's life. Evangelism is a ministry of the entire body of Christ, functioning well. I like to use the example of a dot-to-dot picture, but I will explain this further in another chapter.

While I was writing this chapter, my friend Michele sent me an email update about her ministry. As I read her email, I knew it would fit perfectly with this chapter. I decided to ask her if I could tell you her story, and she said yes. From what I have heard and seen, I believe her giftedness is the gift of mercy. In the weeks preceding my friend's email to me, she had gone out into the country to give a homeless man a ride into town. He was an acquaintance from the homeless community where she serves. As it turned out, this acquaintance brought one of his friends with him, a stranger to Michele. The stranger ended up sitting in the *empty* front *seat* with her. Since they had quite a long ride back to Salem, her gift of mercy started drawing out the stranger's story without any judgment at all, only compassion, while speaking truth. To make a long story short, before they got to town, with a tear running down his cheek, this man, an absolute stranger, asked Jesus to be his Savior. As I said earlier, mercy came running. In that same email, Michele told me of a neighbor she had also led to Christ after he had broken his hip and been in rehab. The gift of God's mercy in my friend squirts out in every direction from her life's message as He reaches through her, touching the world around her.

One can easily see this gift in Michele's ministry with the homeless on the streets of Salem, Oregon. For a decade, she, along with a faithful, godly lady friend, has been serving and loving people toward Christ on those streets, independently and at their own expense. As a result of their faithful effort, my friend's church, located right across the street from the primary area where the homeless gather during the day, has become sensitized to this needy group of neighbors. The leadership of this large city church is now providing a place out of which to serve, plus additional help and some funds. What I find even more exciting is that the pastor of this church took it upon himself to preach a series of messages to his congregation about ministering to this group of neighbors who hang out directly across the street from the church. As a result of this pastor's commitment to addressing this need in their community, other city pastors began to hear he was preaching on the subject of ministering to the needy and homeless, and they invited him to speak to them about what he has learned.

Now, how many different kinds of gifts did my friend have to have for all of these evangelistic outreaches to be accomplished? Just the one she was given. God used her consistent, faithful mercy toward ignored and sometimes unlovely people to move His people in that church and then spread out the message into other churches. God also used her gift to evangelize when talking with the stranger in the front seat of her car and in the case of the man in rehab. I believe with my whole being that God wants to use every believer, with their unique life message and their divinely given spiritual gift, to be part of His evangelistic message of seeking and saving those who are lost. We must be faithful and willing to be genuinely used by Him. I will say, emphatically, there is no greater joy than the grace of being used by God!

Since I live inside my own life message and know my own life best, let me wrap up this chapter by applying these truths to what I have seen, from the inside, of God using me over the years. I believe I have the single gift of wisdom. I define wisdom as a gift to untangle knots or direct people out of the maze they find themselves in. That is the approach I take when someone fills the *empty seat* that God places near me. I start asking questions with what I called in an earlier chapter bifurcated listening. I ask questions and listen to the answers with my ears while my spirit listens for God's insights. If or when God gives insight through His gift in me, I follow that lead as far as God will let me go.

As you might imagine, this same spiritual gift works well for me in counseling. I find that God, using the gift He has given me through my individual life message, gives me the ability to untangle knots and help people find their way. It has also served me well in my role with churches dead in the water and asking for help to figure out what should be next for them. Also, when I preach, I have found that complex and even apparently convoluted passages of scripture have not held me back because God uses that gift in me to untangle the perceived knots in the text. The same gift has given me insight into starting churches or parallel Christian organizations to those churches. People ask me how I can stand constantly working with people or organizations in crisis, but it is not a burden for me, in actuality. And that is because I am operating in the wheelhouse of my spiritual gift and life message.

On the flip side, I do not do mercy. I am useless at helps or

service. I have tried, but I am usually in the way. Also, I have
never had to sell tickets to hear my teaching, and on other occasions, I have come out of meetings thinking I had been encouraging and uplifting, only to find out that I left someone in a
puddle of tears. It is definitely not that I disdain these gifts; I
watch in wonder as God uses them through other believers in
my world. I also know from the scriptures that each area of giftedness mentioned is a part of the believer's toolbox in life. Each
of these categories, be it showing mercy, or being an encouragement, or serving others, is mentioned in the scriptures as part
of what we *all* should be willing to do when called on to be or
do. But as a spiritual gift, it is not me. It is not that I am not
willing because I do try to obey the scriptures where such
behavior is needed. But when any of these manifests as a
personalized spiritual gift in someone, it is a beauty to see in
action, and the results can be miraculous.

The concept I have laid out in this chapter could help every
believer see an avenue for sharing their faith. It can be quite
freeing when we know that evangelism is for you and for me,
and it is not just a special gift given only to special people. If,
like my dad, you do not know what your gift is, do not fret
about it. Just serve in several ways while keeping an eye open
for a sweet spot in ministry that brings you joy. If you can, ask a
ministry friend what they have observed of you while serving in
a particular area. If you have a spouse who knows and loves the
Lord, you could even ask what he or she has observed. But most
of all, ask the Lord to give you His insight about your service. I
believe you will find your spiritual gift. God wants you to serve

skillfully and effectively in your gift more than you want to, so if you take the time and make the effort, He will make things clear.

In all of this, I believe you will find a giftedness that could become *your* gift of evangelism, which will be through *your* own spiritual gift. The years of feeling guilty because deep down inside, you knew you should be witnessing but always found yourself believing that you were not an evangelist could be over. It is such a joy when you suddenly realize that God just used you, just as you are, with your specific spiritual gift, and through your individual life message, in a salvific moment. May I leave you with a challenge? Try it. You may just find that being a part of evangelism and maybe even getting to connect that last dot to faith is not as difficult or as daunting as you thought.

CHAPTER 8
SOTERIOLOGY: THE DOCTRINE OF SALVATION

S oteriology, the doctrine of salvation, is a bit of a stretch for a chapter title because it is doubtful there is a more important subject than this in the scriptures, and it is impossible to do this doctrine justice in just one chapter. The doctrine of salvation is worth volumes of attention.

I am, however, going to attempt to throw some light on the subject, the actual moment of salvation, so that we who are soul winners have some understanding of what we are leading individuals toward. I will also endeavor to show some of the work of the Spirit of God in saving a soul and hopefully lessen the pressure of feeling like one does not fully understand their role in the process of evangelism. Quite often, a fear factor for people sharing the gospel is that they will not get that moment right or that they will lead a person to something that sounds good but will not actually save them.

For this reason, we might ask, "What do lost sinners need to know?" or "What do they need to acknowledge?" or "What words should they say, or is it even necessary for them to say words or a prayer for salvation?" These questions all point to the confusion around the moment of salvation. What is confusing is that there are a number of differing statements in scripture regarding the same salvation. When approaching the moment of salvation, we must realize that the scripture does it from different perspectives and in different story lines, using different but appropriate statements for that storyline.

Even though it is made very clear that there is only *one* Door, there are as many paths to get to that Door as there are people who have stepped through the Door. For example, think of the life and path of Nicodemus, compared to the life and path of the woman at the well, compared to life and path of Zacchaeus, compared to the life and path of the man born blind in John chapter 9, just to name a few. Each came out of lives of their own personal confusion to meet Christ, the Door, and step through to eternal life.

In this paragraph, I am going to list a few apparent differing statements from scripture to show how they can be confusing. This leads me to say that if we understand the moment of salvation, we will use the words that the Spirit of Christ gives us for that person, at that moment, without creating a statement of extreme liability because of different terminology. Each of these statements in scripture is true. But the Holy Spirit has customized each statement for the salvation experience of the individual or individuals spoken of in the text. Let's look at each in turn:

- "Everyone who calls on the name of the Lord will be saved."
- "Unless you turn and become as little children, you will by no means enter the kingdom of heaven."
- "You must be born again."
- "But the one who endures to the end will be saved."
- "Repent and be baptized every one of you in the name of Jesus Christ for the forgiveness of your sins and you will receive the gift of the Holy Spirit."
- "But to all who did receive him, who believed in his name, he gave the right to become children of God."
- "Godly sorrow brings repentance that leads to salvation and leaves no regret."
- "If you confess with your mouth that Jesus is Lord and believe in your heart that God raised him from the dead, you will be saved."

Encountering one of these statements, by itself, can seem to contain the entire message of leading a person to Christ. That is, until one encounters another apparently different statement about the act of salvation, and then in another passage, finding yet a different declarative truth. That is why we are looking for the essence of the salvation moment. Each of the statements above is a separate scriptural quote that you can find for yourself. They are all exactly true but reflect the paths of different sinners moving toward and finding the Door.

The Greek word for salvation is "*sozo*," and from it, we get our English word "soteriology," most often relating to the moment of salvation that this chapter is about. Let me give you an example from the Bible of a spiritual journey that leads to *sozo*, or that moment of salvation. Then, applying that Bible story, we will try to learn exactly what that moment entailed. As we look at this passage, I will not take the time to give all the words of the text from Luke 17:12-19. This is the story of the ten lepers that Jesus healed. The story has four keywords that we will look at to move us through the process, or decision, which led to the salvation of the one Samaritan leper. The other nine men could well have been saved later. We do not really know for certain. But we do know about the one leper.

The first of the four words in this passage that I want to draw our attention to is the word in verse 13, "The ten lepers raised their voices and said, 'Jesus, Master, have mercy on us.'" Their cry for mercy here is the general word for mercy, and I do not think there is any evidence in the passage that they are thinking of salvation when they are crying out for Jesus to have mercy on them. After all, their leprosy had brought them to look for Jesus so that they might be healed. It strikes me that, without leprosy, they likely would have been at their villages doing whatever their previous trade might have been, not searching for the Great Physician and His mercy. Their paths to Jesus, the Door, in the recent part of their lives, were directed by the desperateness of leprosy. In all likelihood, these men had heard of the leper that Jesus had touched and healed early on in His ministry. If they had, it might have been the frantic hope spawned by his story that drove them to seek out Jesus. If they had not been men who were ruined for life by leprosy, they would not have been there crying out for Jesus, the Great Physician, who was also the Door, to notice them and heal them.

It is interesting to me that there is no record that Jesus moved physically close to these ten lepers as He did with the earlier leper who was by himself and whom Jesus physically touched. Note in this passage that Jesus just answered these men with a statement. He told them to go and show themselves to the priests, which was the commandment in the Law for lepers who had been healed. We know their obedience to Jesus' statement caused the cleansing to happen because that is how the text is written. The second word that we notice here is "cleansed." Wherever and whenever a leper found himself near people, they were obligated to shout out the word "unclean." So, the word "cleansed" is the best and normal word here. It appears likely that the reputation of Jesus as the Great Healer had brought these men to Jesus. His statement to them to "go" and their obedience to do so resulted in their physical cleansing. But notice something here. Thus far, there is no indication of salvation, at least not based on the words that the Holy Spirit wrote through Luke in this text.

When the text tells us about the one leper who was a Samaritan, and who noticed, "... that he was healed, turned back, praising God..." (verse 15), even here the Greek word is the very normal word for "healing," which is our third word. Now here comes our fourth and most significant word. It is not until after the Samaritan leper falls on his face at the feet of Jesus and gives thanks to Him when Jesus uses a particular word. He said to this one leper, "Your faith has made you well." The word "well" here... are you ready for this? ... is *sozo*, which is our Greek word for *salvation* (verses 16-19). It is clear to me in the text that the leper's surrender at the feet of Jesus is his moment of salvation. Everything leading up to it could be called his spiritual journey or his path to the Door, which culminated in surrender to what he knew about Jesus, which I expect was acknowledging Jesus as the Christ.

My reason for using this story in Luke chapter 17 is to pinpoint the moment of salvation, in juxtaposition to nine other men in very parallel circumstances, to whom Jesus does not declare their faith has saved them. Remember, in the text, it tells us that they were all cleansed and healed, but only the Samaritan leper had Jesus the Christ specifically say to him that his faith had *saved* him, as he surrendered at Jesus' feet. In my understanding and experience, in the life of a lost sinner - in this case, the Samaritan leper - there must come a moment of *surrender* to what one *understands* about salvation, which only comes from Jesus the Christ, surrendering to the only Way, the Door.

In John chapter 14:6, Jesus tells us that He is the way, the truth, and the life, and according to His own words, is the only access to God the Father. Earlier in the book of John (10:9),

Jesus declares, "I am the door. If anyone enters by me, he will be saved...."

Some people have told me this concept of only one door is not fair, or that a simple surrender to the work of Christ is too easy, and there must be more to it. The funny thing is Paul is proven to be precisely right again and again in 1 Corinthians chapters 1 and 2 when he explains that people who view themselves as wise and intelligent have a hard time accepting the simplicity and finality of the moment of salvation. They seem to want to add man-made religious tenants to the moment of salvation. God, in His wisdom, has made it such that a child or an inquirer with no background in Christianity will be able to comprehend and believe as much as a formally trained religious cleric would. I, myself, was only four years old when I was saved for eternity. I had no difficulty comprehending the Cross and substitution, and can remember and relate every part of my surrendering that day to Christ's way of salvation. This was because the teaching in that Good News Club, a week-long evangelistic kids' program, was specific and succinct. The Good News about the message is that it is a level playing field for whoever will come to God through Jesus Christ.

Recently, I learned again how the powerful message of the atonement could be simply taught and received. A few friends and I had a ministry to teenage boys who were almost entirely sons of African immigrants. The church we were using had a gym with a kitchen. This allowed us to serve the young men breakfast, followed by about twenty minutes of me teaching them from God's Word. I had the privilege of weekly presenting to these boys the claims of Christ. After the teaching time, the young men would play basketball. The way the gym was laid out gave me a massive and excellent object lesson regarding the moment of salvation. I used this object lesson repeatedly when inviting the boys to receive Christ as their Savior. The boys we were working with ranged in age from eleven to seventeen. When we began ministering to them, most of them did not even know what Easter and Christmas were all about. Because of this, my huge object lesson was an excellent tool in this context.

The illustration worked like this: One wall of the gym, which was two stories high and about eighty feet long, had four openings through it. On the far end of one side, an opening went up to a second-floor by way of a long, straight, steep staircase. The next opening was a door into the kitchen, followed by double doors into a storage place for folding tables and chairs. Down on the other end, there were double doors with crash bars on them. These doors led straight to the outside as an emergency exit.

Using the above scriptures (in John 10 and 14) about Jesus being the Door and the only way to God, I explained it this way: "Imagine that God and Heaven are in the kitchen, and the nice lady that fixed you breakfast this morning was one of the angels. The Bible says there's only one way, one Door to God, through His Son, Jesus, and what He did on the Cross." I would then talk with them about what other religions and other theories taught about how to access God. I would use the other openings in the walls of that gymnasium, pointing out that these other openings would not gain them access to the kitchen (my example of Heaven and where God was). In addition to the other openings through the wall, I would pretend to try and climb the wall to get over it or attempted to kick a hole through it or bang my head against it, all of which did not succeed in gaining access to God in the kitchen. I would illustrate that there were many paths to get to the gym, but there was only one door leading into the kitchen once in the gym. After all this teaching theater, I would explain that it took swallowing pride and having a spirit of surrender to say that the apparently insignificant door near the middle of the wall was the only way, and then pass through it. This illustration was simple and straightforward because the essence of the Good News is straightforward and simple too.

Based on my conversations with some of the boys each week, when I gave them an opportunity to tell God that they surrender to His way, the only way, I believe that most of them made that decision one time or another during those couple of years. Because of the cultural differences, I did not push them for any show of hands, but I gave them opportunities to pray with me if they agreed with what I was saying. Quite often, when I closed the prayer of invitation, boys would audibly agree with an "Amen." Even though circumstances ended my involvement in that ministry, and I moved on to other ministries, I still pray for each one of them because I know that the Spirit of God will continue to work in them through other people and events in their lives (Philippians 1:6).

The point I am making here is that God is not willing that

any should perish. He will not make the path or door to salvation a thing that's complex and almost unattainable. The Holy Spirit is actively engaged in drawing individual people toward Himself simply by using many things from that person's world and the universe itself in this process. We read this in Romans 1:19-20,

> For what can be known about God is plain to them, because God has shown it to them. For his invisible attributes, namely, his eternal power and divine nature, have been clearly perceived, ever since the creation of the world, in the things that have been made. So they are without excuse.

In addition to this, scripture assures us that each person has their own awareness of God because "...he has put eternity into man's heart..." (Ecclesiastes 3:11). We always assume the worst about the lost person in front of us, forgetting that behind their facade of resistance, God has been and is at work drawing them to Himself. The Spirit of God knows the way to the individual's heart and will prompt our use of words, illustrations, and scripture while He engages them through us. Far more people in our world are ready to respond to the gospel than there are those of us who are willing to engage them toward that end.

In the Gospels, we see Jesus keeping the message simple using straightforward illustrations like seed and sower, birds, the grass in the field, trees, and mountains to explain His claims as Christ. He stated simple, straightforward eternal truth and rarely argued doctrine. Too often, a confused believer will do the opposite by wasting time arguing with an unbeliever about moral behavior, or politics, or evolution, or that a person should go to church, or that they should receive the Spirit, or that one religion or another is better, or that they should just love everyone, or forgive and make amends, and the list goes on. Obviously, each of these is a good thing, but the witnessing believer needs to point the lost sinner toward the essence of gospel truth, which is surrendering to the work of Jesus Christ as the only way. This surrender will include an individualized level of repentance. It may even involve remorse and/or declarations of change like those of Zacchaeus when he told Jesus, at the moment of his salvation, that he would give half of everything he owned to the poor. I believe, however, that this essence of the gospel is the surrender to what God calls "the atonement," accompanied by words to God spoken out loud or in their inner person.

Many people today, however, make the message even more complex by objecting to the practice of using words, such as a prayer, for stepping through this Door to eternal life, and for some reason, there are even those that will use sarcastic comments to put down prayer at the moment of salvation. These individuals will describe a prayer for salvation by saying pejorative things, denigrating heartfelt prayers as just magic words or a magic formula. Possibly this attitude comes from the misuse of popular tracts used during the second half of the twentieth century. In those days, and even somewhat today, witnessing tools such as little hand-out gospel tracts included a prayer on the back page. They helped the one witnessing to lead the sinner in praying as the act of crossing into eternal life. Simple prayers for salvation are also still being used today in radio, TV ads, and podcasts, endeavoring to give a brief message of salvation, sometimes in as little time as sixty seconds. I do not believe there is anyone who would argue that this is the best and most effective form of personal evangelism, but there are still souls being saved by using these techniques. We should not discount the sincere prayer of a sinner receiving grace because we do not like the prayer of salvation used. I challenge the right of anyone to have the spiritual and moral authority to speak in a demeaning way and to judge the soul winning effort of any Christian individual or ministry, which includes the words of a prayer for salvation. I respect any child of God's effort who is at least trying to reach the lost in their community. I so wish that I was exaggerating this point, but I'm afraid I am not. This attitude seems to be pervasive, and it is destructive. Let's see for ourselves what the scripture says about using words spoken to God as the means to enter through the Door of salvation.

Jesus makes statements, throughout the Gospels, regarding the use of words when it comes to spiritual surrender and belief. In Matthew 12:36, 37, He says this about the importance of the use of words at the day of judgment: "But I say to you that for every idle word men may speak, they will give account of it in the day of judgment. For by your words you will be justified, and by your words you will be condemned" (NJKV). In Luke 12:8, while speaking to a very large and diverse crowd, He said, "...whoever confesses Me before men, him the Son of Man also will confess before the angels of God" (NKJV). Throughout the Gospels, we see Jesus pushing individuals in different ways to use words to identify their belief in Him.

One of my favorite examples is Jesus' face-to-face encounter with the man born blind in John 9:35-38.

> Jesus heard that they had cast him out; and when He had found him, He said to him, "Do you believe in the Son of God" He answered and said, "Who is He, Lord, that I may believe in Him?" And Jesus said to him, "You have both seen Him and it is He who is talking with you." Then he said, "Lord, I believe!" And he worshiped Him. (NKJV)

In Jesus' encounter with the blind individual in John 9, we get some idea of the man's journey leading up to the moment of belief. We then see his belief, surrender in worship, and words proclaiming his belief. The apostle Paul, later in Romans 10, teaches something similar when he ties verbal confession very closely with faith and being saved. Look here at verses 8-10:

> But what does it say? "The word is near you, in your mouth and in your heart" (that is, the word of faith that we proclaim); because, if you confess with your mouth that Jesus is Lord and believe in your heart that God raised him from the dead, you will be saved. For with the heart one believes and is justified, and with the mouth one confesses and is saved.

Later in chapter 10, still speaking about the moment of salvation, he says in verse 13, "For everyone who calls on the name of the Lord will be saved."

For a couple of years, I had been speaking with Dwight, an African American recovering addict, about a relationship with Jesus that would solidify his recovery. At one point, he ended up in a hospital for a few days, fighting for his life because of an injury. When I showed up in his hospital room, after he had come out of intensive care, I walked in the door of his room and sat on the edge of his bed. Then I asked him, "Dwight, are you ready yet to surrender to what Jesus has done and will do for you?" He did not answer in the way I expected. He just began praying out loud, telling God he was a hopeless, lousy sinner and that he could never make it to Heaven any other way. He asked God to take his soul and make something of it. In short, Dwight called on the name of the Lord and was saved. His prayer included surrender to the work of Christ, and he spoke his desire for salvation in *words*. I had never spoken to him about praying a sinner's prayer. His ready heart, however, knew exactly what to do. Dwight was marvelously saved, and for many years I considered him one of my best friends. He eventually died because of complications from the earlier injury. So, yes, his prayer was magical and from his heart. His words to God were his complete surrender to Him, which saved Dwight, giving him eternal life in the presence of God.

Dwight's prayer begs the question: Must the words that a lost sinner says to God in surrender be audible? No, of course not. Words spoken in the heart and mind to God are also the real thing. Any words spoken or thought to God are prayers. When dealing with a lost soul who may have no experience with God and prayer, it often helps to suggest the type of thing he or she might want to say to God in surrendering to Him, like the one I spoke of earlier written at the end of an evangelistic tract. In most such situations, a person will tell the evangelist that he does not know how to pray or what to say. At this point, it is entirely appropriate to ask him if he would like you to suggest words in a prayer, and if he agrees that what you are saying is what he is thinking, then he should repeat the words after you. Sometimes he or she will repeat the words aloud and sometimes will repeat them silently in his or her heart and mind.

There is so much more that could be discussed about prayer when we think of all that is involved in the circumstances of a lost individual's journey toward salvation as Christ draws each to Himself. In this chapter, however, we have been exclusively discussing the moment of salvation as I see it in the scripture. My goal is to clarify the perspective that the soul winner needs to have. This gives confidence in knowing and believing what the crucial point a lost sinner must get to in receiving salvation is. It helps us understand what kind of declaration to God will give that soul confidence in his or her salvation experience. In the future, when the devil tries to make them doubt, as new believers, this inner confidence from their experience of surrender will help them defeat that doubt. Remember, I am just talking with you about a smidgen of the overall doctrine called soteriology.

Each believer, symbolically, has an *empty seat* we need to pray for God to fill for His kingdom. That could be someone who may sit next to you on a plane, or at a lunch table, or on a train, or a bus, or a coworker, or a family member who needs the Lord. During the pandemic, when fellow Christians would bemoan not being out there on the frontlines of ministry because of the shutdown, I told them that God had moved the front lines to the edge of their own property. Their neighbors were on this new front and needed the Lord. What about your neighbors, and what about mine? We must engage with them. Some of them, maybe even many of them, are already being prepared for salvation by the Holy Spirit. We must connect the dots and see what God will do.

Whether you are a mature Christian, a church leader, a student formally studying for the ministry, or maybe a discouraged believer, I am writing this book intending to help you grasp the simplicity of leading someone to that point of surrendering to Jesus Christ. You and I do not have the option of giving up on Christ's mandate to be active in the purpose of the body of Christ, to seek and to save that which is lost. Perhaps, if we have a clearer understanding that there needs to be a moment of surrender, it might just help encourage us not to give up but instead to watch for Spirit-prompted opportunities. There is no greater joy than to be part of that salvation moment in someone's life.

CHAPTER 9
THE ROLE OF FAITH IN SALVATION/INVISIBLE MADE VISIBLE

A lot is made of faith in most cultures because every person believes in something, even if it is just their ability to disagree with everything. Religions demand faith in something, but it is not always just in their idea of God. They often demand belief in the religion itself, spiritual leaders, or the efficaciousness of rituals or relics. Every religion makes claims that the acts of faith in their system will allow you to appease God, who might then let you into its concept of paradise, that is, every religion except biblical Christianity. It is only biblical Christianity that points toward a God who is Love and a God who is seeking us. He is a God who not only seeks us but is a God who desires that no one, anywhere, should perish! What is more, the God of Christianity delights in His created humanity and desires every person to spend eternity with Him in Heaven. Eternal salvation and pleasing Him depend only on believing what He has revealed and then receiving His love.

If you think about it, salvation is an entirely invisible condition believed in and received. This all works because a lost soul becomes aware of the potential of invisible forgiveness from an invisible God. Then this condition of forgiveness of sins comes to the individual by faith, which is heart-surrender to the work of Jesus on the Cross. This act of Christ on the Cross is also not visible to the sinner because, of course, it took place 2000 years ago. It becomes believed in when an open heart sees visual, living evidence and hears the truth explained. As soul winners, we need to understand that salvation is invisible; it will never be accessed by visible deeds of religious homage but only by faith. Though invisible, faith is distinctly powerful by being essential for salvation. Hebrews 11:6 says that without faith, it is impossible to please God.

This saving faith is so powerful that we cannot possibly muster enough of it to save ourselves. Although, as humans, we try by looking for a feeling that we can identify as faith or even a heroic act of dedication that will put us in a spiritually safe place. None of that works, however, for God Himself must give salvation as a gift. "For by grace you have been saved through faith. And this is not your own doing; it is the gift of God, not a result of works..." (Ephesians 2:8-9). At this point of spiritual tenderness, religions of all kinds find it irresistible to add visible deeds of obeisance to try and make the act of salvation feel good. The unadulterated truth is that, at the point of salvation, when a lost soul finally gets to the point of surrender, God gives that person a gift. This gift is the powerful faith to believe, carrying him or her across the threshold and through the Door of eternal life.

If salvation itself is invisible, and the faith that accomplishes that salvation is also invisible, and if lost individuals live life expecting absolutely nothing from an invisible God, how will a lost individual come to desire a relationship with Christ and find that faith that saves? The answer lies in this fact: God designed the *results* of saving faith to be completely visible. Let me show you how this works. It works through the tangible and verbal witness of a visibly changed and changing life, one who has already received God's gift. These living witnesses of invisible salvation are the born-again believers living victorious lives, clearly seen in the same world as their lost family and friends. In other words, we Christians make the invisible, divine presence visible through the Holy Spirit in our lives. Some call this being an image bearer, meaning that the Spirit of Christ becomes seen as the image of Christ in the character and life of a practicing Christian.

There are two primary dimensions of making the invisible visible. I will explain them in this chapter. Both of these only work when walking by faith, drenched in prayer, and through intentional salvific relationships by believers with their lost family and friends. God, of course, has provided for this by giving each of us a spiritual gift that we can use in evangelizing. The apostle Paul says that each of us, through the gift of God in our lives, makes the Holy Spirit visible or manifest (1st Corinthians 12:7).

Do you remember those dot-to-dot pictures from your childhood? The final picture was not complete in those pages until dot number one connected to dot number two, all the way through until the last line was drawn to the last dot. Then, and then only, was the picture complete. The first helpful understanding in soul winning is similar to a dot-to-dot picture. A saving knowledge of Jesus often comes about similarly. It is when a believer begins connecting dots for a lost soul by their Christian character and occasionally adding verbal witness. In this way, they make the need to be saved relevant through living their lives out loud, and clarifying the truth with words, when God gives the opportunity.

When examining the process of salvation for most individuals, one notices that often there had been many believers who had taken their turn connecting dots as the picture of Christ formed for that lost soul. In the formation of the picture of Christ, every dot connected, from the first dot to the last dot, was a believer using the message of their life and some well-timed words, through their individual spiritual gifting, to connect the dot in front of them. Sometimes the individual believer is connecting the first two dots of someone's concept of the Savior. Then other times, God may bring in other believers to connect the next dots, all the way through the picture until the final Christian comes along and gets to connect the last dot, making the picture of Jesus fully visible and clear.

Most of the time, we don't know which dots in the picture of Christ we are connecting, but by faith, we believe that God fully understands the role He wants us to play, and that will be the dot He sets before us. However, when that last person gets to connect the final dots, that one has the joy of experiencing the moment when the unsaved individual, at last, sees the full picture and realizes it is Jesus he or she needs to save his or her soul. It is then that the believer can lead that unsaved person to the point of saving faith, or surrender. My encouragement to you is this: seldom will God give us the entire job of cultivating the whole picture of Christ for a person that God is drawing to Himself. I encourage you to think of it this way, just connect the dots in front of you. Do not push past what is available, and do not stop if the opportunity is still in front of you. It has always been God's job to save. We just have the privilege of participating in His work by faith, connecting the dots that He gives us to connect.

Isn't this a guilt-relieving concept? Let me reiterate because this concept is crucial. You and I have only to connect the dots that are right in front of us and keep on praying. We do not have to panic about taking a lost soul through to the fully visible picture of Christ for their lives or panic about "closing the deal," even if the person is our own contact. People are not our projects, especially when it comes to their salvation. The forever-act of salvation is God's problem and His alone. We are given the privilege of being part of the process of making saving truth relevant and visible, one dot at a time until the image of Christ becomes fully visible.

In this process of connecting dots in the life of the lost soul, besides prayer, there are three identifiable phases that God may have any one of us participate in by faith. These three phases comprise the second helpful understanding I mentioned earlier. The initials for these three happen to be *IRS*, which stands for *Introduction, Relevance,* and *Surrender.* When connecting dots, you could be doing any of these three.

Rod and I were sitting in the front row seats of the 737. The seat between us was empty, but I doubted that it would remain that way since the front row seldom remains open. Rod's first words turned out to be antagonistic. He leaned over the seat between us and asked, "I see you're wearing a cross. Does that mean you're a Christian?" The conversation went downhill from there. I asked God to keep that seat between us empty so that we could talk, which He did. Let me abbreviate our discussion by saying that Rod thought all Christians were hypocrites and that the Bible, which he claimed to know much better than most Christians did, was a joke and full of stupid statements and errors. He waxed eloquently about how well educated he was as a retired banker, and that Hell was a ridiculous concept, and that the only hell was what people made for themselves. I listened and drew him out on his thoughts about Christianity, letting him vent until he blew out all his steam. After all, God had given me a captive audience for two-and-a-half hours, from Denver to Seattle. God kept the middle seat empty for His purpose.

There were several statements Rod made that I was able to give some level of agreement to. For example, I told him that the Greek definition of hypocrite was actually putting a mask in front of one's face to hide behind. He liked that and made a note of it to put in his argument arsenal. I agreed that, by that definition, most Christians were hypocrites at least some of the time and that this included me. As Christians, I explained that we are very aware we're sinners who are saved for Heaven but are still working out our problems here on earth, and that is why we go to church. Churches are places that help us identify our weaknesses and help us to work them out. I asked him what scripture he thought taught Christians that they were perfect. He said he'd have to think about that. I asked him who it was in his world who claimed to be a Christian and claimed to be perfect. He couldn't remember.

I told him I agreed that many people make their own kind of hell for themselves on Earth. I also told him that I didn't personally like the teaching about Hell, but that each person has to decide for themselves if they agree with, not like, but agree with the doctrine of an eternal Hell. My approach in times like these is to be as agreeable as possible but to get essential truths into the person's mind in the *empty seat* to think about it later.

Finally, we began the approach to Seattle, having gone north and west around Mount Rainier and now coming in over the city. I have been told that, when flying that route past the top part of the mountain, you feel like you can reach out and touch it. Rod commented about the view and then saw my white cane in the holder in front of me. He became embarrassed and very apologetic, saying that he was sorry for his comments because he didn't know I was blind. I assured him that being blind made no difference to our discussion and that I did not consider myself blind, but that, based on truth in the scripture, God had given me a slightly different role in life. It was to manage life from inside a blind body. Rod was silent for a while, leaning over and looking at the incredible view. Shortly before we landed, he admitted he really didn't know much about the Bible and that, in fact, maybe he'd never really known a Christian. He went on to say the following, which is the point of this story. He said, "Harry, if you're what a Christian is, I think I'll take another look at Christ and Christianity." The time I had with Rod on that flight was Rod's *introduction* to making faith visible, the first dot. I did not attempt to connect any other dots. I had connected the dots in front of me, and the rest of the picture was up to the Lord. I am certain He has taken care of the entire message of salvation for Rod as his life went on. I still pray for him, but the Lord has not allowed our paths to cross again.

On the return flight from Seattle, I was given the privilege of *introducing* again. I was in the same row, on another 737, but in the reversed seating arrangement. The seat between myself and a young college student named Doug remained vacant by God's grace, once again. While Doug was in Seattle on a break from a university in Denver, he had been in a long-boarding accident. Now, he was in a foot-to-hip cast, and he almost bragged about the details of his long-board catastrophe. At some point, I asked him if he considered himself to be a spiritual person, to which he enthusiastically answered, "Yes." I drew him out as to what that meant to him and then asked him what his spiritual sensibilities told him about what would have happened to him if that which was crushed on his body had been his head and if that which was broken had been his neck. His answer was all over the place. Finally, he said, "Honestly, I don't know what would've happened." He then asked me, from my perspective, what did *I* think happens when a person dies. After my explanation, he said, "I need to think about that." He then put his seat back and took a nap. Later, while getting ready to deplane, Doug said that it must be hard to be blind. He then thanked me again for the conversation and told me that he'd never given life after death much thought but that he would sincerely think about it now. Again, this was *introduction* and connecting initial dots.

Outside of prayer, probably the most important part of connecting dots comes out of the believers' ongoing faith walk before the lost. This is what I call *relevance*. This could be a short period, or it could be a lifetime. By living as Christ's image joyfully, peacefully, and with contentment, a believer shows the unsaved person who is in their life that salvation is real. Their life makes the message of the gospel relevant rather than ethereal. One's life, plus words, when God allows them, connect more dots beyond just the *introduction,* which then begins to make the picture of Christ more evident, leading toward the goal of helping unbelievers realize they need Him as their Savior. I have many true stories of how individuals have exquisitely contributed to the salvation of their loved ones by connecting dots that have made Christ relevant and visible.

Let me tell you about two women from the same church who marvelously exemplified the *relevance* of Christ to their unsaved husbands by being image-bearers. One wife, Becky, had to wait and watch and pray for years. The other wife, Wendy, saw her husband's salvation in just two months after her own salvation experience. Becky came to know Christ as her Savior before we started a church in her neighborhood. When she began attending the church plant, I told her I would work with her in supplicating for the salvation of Troy, her husband. Becky grew and grew in the Lord and endeavored to live the Christ-life and values in front of her children and husband. Every time I asked her about Troy, she would tell me there was no sign of spiritual movement in his life. You see, Troy was a good ol' boy and a man's man. Even though he had been drinking heavily since his youth and had then expanded into cocaine, he was still holding down a good job. He loved fishing, sports, and gambling and was very lost. Becky prayed faithfully while continuing to walk the walk. I prayed faithfully and continued to hold out hope on her behalf. She had essentially lost hope that he would ever be interested in Christ, seeing no noticeable change in his attitudes despite her living out Christ's relevance in her life.

One afternoon, towards the end of the workday, Troy proved Becky wrong and the principle of *relevance* right. Everyone else in the church building had left, and my secretary was on her way out of the door to her car when she noticed a parked pickup truck across the parking lot. Sitting in it was a man who appeared to be watching the door of the office. She came back in to tell me about him and to ask if she should stay. I told her to go ahead and go home and that I would be all right. Five minutes after she drove away, I heard the front door of the office open, and this man from the truck, whom I had never met, came in and introduced himself as Troy. After we were seated in my office, his message was short and sweet. While choking up, he told me that Becky was the most amazing woman on Earth and that he was unworthy of her. He went on to ask if there was any way that *he* could know God as she did. Not only had her walk made the fruits of salvation visible and relevant, but it had brought him to the point of surrender to the work of Christ on the Cross, and that is what he did that afternoon. This response took years of Becky making visible the Christ-life before Troy realized it was Jesus that he needed to surrender his life to.

Wendy, on the other hand, saw her husband Owen's salvation just a couple of months after she surrendered her life to Christ. This is their story. Wendy, through what was clearly a small miracle happening in her life, was led to come and see me in my office. She knew nothing about me or the church, but God had directed her through that miraculous event to come and meet with me. That afternoon, after explaining what she felt was a miracle, I had the privilege of connecting the last dot in the picture that God had already been working on, and Wendy was truly saved. God had already done the heavy lifting; I just closed the deal with her. She told me how Owen had left her and the kids and had run off with one of his young, female employees, and they were somewhere in a cocaine-induced fantasy land. He would still come by the house periodically, not to stay long, but just to get clothes or food.

As Wendy grew in the Lord, she began learning to pray and how to walk by faith and live the Christ-life all the time, even when Owen was at home. She trusted, and God provided. When Owen asked how she was surviving, she told him that God, through a thing called salvation, was changing her. He gave no regard to what she was saying, or at least that is the way it seemed to Wendy. But one afternoon, near the end of the day, Owen showed up at my office unannounced just as Troy had done. He said, "Reverend, I have to talk to you." Before I could get him seated in my office, he told me that he was Wendy's husband and that she had,

" ...found something called salvation." He went on to say that he had to have that salvation Wendy had. I introduced him to the only One who could give it to him, and Owen was forgiven and born again right then and there. In the very short time of two months, Wendy's faith and changing life had made the Good News visible and *relevant*. All I did was guide Owen to Jesus Christ, the Door, followed by his personal *surrender* to the work of Christ on the Cross.

Becky and Wendy's Christian walk of faith made Christ visible and the gospel *relevant* to their husbands. *Surrender,* however, was these guys' act of faith, accepting what Jesus had done on the Cross as being the way for their salvation. The wives could not surrender for their husbands, and obviously, neither could I. Relevant faith in Christ Jesus is best explained in actions and clarified in words. Both of these accomplish *introductions* and *relevance* and lead to the point of faith and *surrender*. When a believer is using words to connect dots as God gives the opportunity, that person needs to go as far as God allows, but no further, because the one who is lost must respond individually, with each one's free will, to each one's faith in the work of Christ. As one who bears Christ's image, we must not try to force a response, because Christ never did that to us or anyone else. It is the free will that He gave us to exercise in this decision that will allow the one we are praying for to someday have his or her own fellowship with God Himself, as an image-bearer. Our walk of faith while connecting dots will most often be *introduction* or *relevance*, but *surrender* is the province of the soul finding Christ.

There is, however, another major perspective of faith in the process of people being born again that we need to talk about. I have spoken about the faith of the lost soul to surrender for salvation. I have also spoken of the role of faith in the life of a believer who desires to see someone they know or love be saved, faith that is acted upon by the believer living the Christ-life out loud. This additional perspective on faith, however, also leads to the salvation of another through prayer, obedience, and expectations. The expectations are that God wants that salvation more than they do, and therefore He will work through believers and His Word and circumstances to give the lost soul every opportunity to surrender to the Good News. We can learn this through Hebrews 11:1, where scripture defines faith. I admit this verse can be a rather confusing definition of faith, no matter what translation a person is looking at, so I will give you *my* paraphrase of Hebrews 11:1 as I have understood its definition. "Faith is what you expect of and from God." Let me tell you another story that will show you how this works.

Cliff was a pastor in a small town in the Northwest. He,

along with his church, invited my wife Carol and me to do a mini-conference that I called "Pressing the Restart Button." It was an event that ran on Thursday and Friday evenings, all day Saturday, and Sunday through noon. We would deal with many of the same principles contained in this book. Before our first evening meeting, I sat across the desk from Cliff with his personal library from floor to ceiling on three sides of him. His certificates for his bachelor's degree in Bible and his master's degree in Theology were boldly posted one above the other on one of the only free spaces on the wall. In my desire to know him and his church, I asked about his ministry life, and this startling fact came out. After more than twenty years of ministry, with training from the best theological institutions in the west, Cliff had never led a single person to Christ. He hoped that perhaps someone had heard him preach and figured out their need for a Savior, but he had only given two invitations for salvation in his entire ministry. Further inquiry revealed that he grew up in a church where he had never heard of anyone getting saved, except for children in their homes or Good News Clubs. To be fair to Cliff, he had invited us to come to his church because he longed for something better, but his personal ministry experience had left him with confusion, resulting in negligible expectations to see people saved. On the flip side, no thanks to myself, having been raised in ministry in Africa as I have described, I had fully embedded expectations that God is eager to save the lost and that there are many more people prepared to respond to the Good News than there are believers willing to engage the lost with the gospel.

As startling as this fact about Cliff was, I have learned since then that this is not at all uncommon in the Christian world. Men preparing for ministry are trained to study and preach the Bible, but some never catch any passion for souls, neither from their formal theological training nor from their home churches. Some never understand they are to have expectations of God that people will be saved through their ministry. This is where my definition of faith comes in. First, Hebrews 11:6 says that without faith we cannot please God, and verse one, according to my paraphrase, faith is what we expect from God. So, if we expect next-to-nothing from God, that is what we will get, and we certainly will not please God in the process. This is so very sad because God has clearly stated in passages like Matthew 18:14 that, "So it is not the will of your Father who is in heaven that one of these little ones should perish."

Not only is it true for pastors that they ought to expect to see people saved, but every believer should expect to see people saved. God is not willing that any should perish, and we must believe that fact.

We must conclude that faith is involved in salvation, both on the part of the soul winner who has the expectation that God wants to save and expects that God will use him or her as His witness, and that faith is also a component in saving the lost when they believe and surrender. Another important point is this: prayer and faith are inseparable in salvation. I pointed out earlier that prayer is the believer's basic daily act of faith. Faith and prayer are different sides of the same coin. They are the coin of the realm, the coin of the Kingdom.

Remember the passage in Hebrews 11? It tells us that without faith it is impossible to please God, and with prayer and faith being inseparable, I have to wonder why people think they can see God work in the life of a loved one without regularly supplicating on their behalf. Or why they think they can please God in ministry without talking to God about what He wants to do. Saving souls is God's work, and He is not willing that any should perish. We are, however, God's hands and feet, and He has chosen to use people, made in His image, to make everything about His salvation visible, and we need to, by faith, expect Him to do it.

CHAPTER 10
THE SPREAD OF THE GOSPEL

He put another parable before them saying, "The kingdom of
heaven is like a grain of mustard seed that a man took and
sowed in his field. It is the smallest of all seeds, but when it
has grown it is larger than all the garden plants and becomes a
tree, so that the birds of the air come and make nests in its
branches." He told them another parable. "The kingdom of
heaven is like leaven that a woman took and hid in three
measures of flour, till it was all leavened." (Matthew 13:31-33)

The gospel of God's kingdom is designed to spread and
expand as seen above and in many other scriptures. Jesus
not only spoke and lived and taught this truth, but he also
commanded a response to it. It is never spoken of as being
optional or an issue of personal preference. Spreading the
gospel is commanded and expected as seen in what we call the

Great Commission (Matthew 28:19). For this expansion and spreading of the gospel to *not* happen, it requires disobedience on the part of Christ's Church. Sadly, I have to say I believe that in much of the Church today, it is *not* happening. Whether you agree with this conclusion that it is not happening in much of the Church today or not, we each need to acknowledge the fact that the gospel is meant to be spread, as found in all the teachings of Jesus and His apostles. Then you and I need to act according to their teachings in the scripture. Notice in the parables above how the gospel is not only designed to grow and spread, but in each example, there is human participation in starting that growth and spread.

In this chapter, I will show you some things about gospel growth and spread and tell some stories of the people planting the gospel. I will also show you some of the history and geography of the great story of spreading the kingdom of God.

In the first half of the 1930s, in a small town in the upper peninsula of Michigan, a village evangelist named Dick Zoet felt called to preach the gospel but found nothing but resistance from the two mainline churches that dominated the town. Denied a place to preach by both churches, he turned to the school master and was granted, for a fee, a large classroom to hold meetings in for two weeks. The evangelistic crusade began small. Dick was going to preach the gospel, understanding that it would be God's problem to fill the *empty seats*. On the second night, Mrs. Dagmar Olsen and two of her sons, Ivan and Marlin, were saved. During the remainder of the two weeks, two more of Dagmar's five sons and her daughter made a profession of faith. However, her husband and eldest son resisted the gospel at this point in their lives. Now, I never personally met the Evangelist Dick Zoet, but Dagmar's son, Marlin, is my dad, and he was truly born again at that little crusade, as was his older brother Ivan.

My story of the natural spread and growth of the gospel began with Dick Zoet and continues with these two men. God used both Ivan Olsen and Marlin Olsen to start church movements. The one movement started by Ivan was in Nebraska and all over the western United States, and the other movement by my dad Marlin, was in the southern half of Africa. I am writing this part of the book while sitting in a room on a conference grounds in Nebraska. The church group Dr. Ivan Olsen started, bought this land and built structures on it to service their sixty-some churches.

While the church movement in Nebraska and its surrounding areas grew, I was growing up and attending camp in Africa, in one or the other of the campgrounds that my dad, Marlin Olsen, started. The church movement in Africa continued to expand, too. Dad planted dozens of churches in two countries. With the help of national church leaders and some missionaries, he and my mom started three Bible colleges in Africa. These are still serving the church there. Upon my dad's death, the church in South Africa surveyed the pastors and churches and found that over 70 percent of the pastors preaching in those churches were led to the Lord directly by my father or by someone he had led to the Lord. The church group leader estimated that my dad had personally led roughly a thousand men to the Lord in that country and personally discipled many of them. Now, I do not know that much about the stories behind my dad's brother, Dr. Ivan Olsen's ministry, but I do know that the legacy of Ivan in the US would read much the same way.

I want to, for a moment, expand on the ministry of my dad's life because I know more of it. The point I am making with this storyline should be obvious, showing the gospel's spread with a single humble starting place. Because of God's grace, you will see the story has not ended, nor will it, for generations to come. In our family alone, as a part of this spread and growth of the gospel, my sister Mary Beth became a Christian counselor and ministered in Christian women's shelters, constantly spreading the Good News. In addition to that, she taught and oversaw regions of ministry through Child Evangelism Fellowship. My brother Ted has served for years, training indigenous individuals to go and start churches with unreached people groups. Thousands have been saved through his efforts, and many churches have been planted where the Kingdom keeps spreading. As for me, my wife Carol and I have spent our entire adult lives starting or restarting churches, or overseeing the launching of other churches here in the US, and filling *empty seats* at the banquet table in Heaven. And, as you can see from the true stories in this book, the grace of God has allowed us to be used by Him to directly spread the gospel of salvation. And out of all these churches in our ministry, there have been those who have gone on to be successful in taking the *next* generation of the Kingdom's message to *other* parts of the world.

None of us who are mentioned in this narrative are anywhere near super saints. Our spouses and friends would laugh out loud at such a concept. We all have rough edges and have functioned strictly by the grace of God alone. That, however, is the point. Regular people, rough and sometimes wrong about things, are all that God has to use. Only Jesus was always right and perfect in every way. I guess all of this begs the "What if?" question. What if Dick Zoet didn't obey God and hold a little crusade in that small insignificant village in the upper peninsula of Michigan, sowing the mustard seed of the Kingdom? I am certain the world would be a much darker place now. We must remember that it takes a very human person to plant the mustard seed, or the lump of leaven, but the perfect God makes it spread and spread and spread, and grow and grow and grow.

Let's talk for a few moments about the history of the faith and the heroes of faith that spread the Kingdom news in past generations. The following timeline should help us in this discussion. Remember that *time* is a creation of God in eternity. It does not change eternity, but eternity engulfs it in incomprehensible ways. The story of time steps to the foreground in God's eternal plan, with Paradise in the first two chapters of the Bible, and then ends time as we know it with Paradise-to-come in the last two chapters of the Bible. That which is between the Paradise we read of in Genesis 1 and 2 and Paradise-to-come in Revelation 21 and 22 is the swamp of fallen humanity. The Bible covers this time by showing the need for a Redeemer and offering the background and backstory of that Redeemer. It then shows the redemption, the power of redemption, and the Redeemer, culminating with the final victory of the Redeemer King. This story of redemption causes certain individuals and groups to rise above the swamp of humanity as they serve God's purpose of redeeming humanity from its self-imposed fall from grace. These biblical characters are the heroes of the faith during their eras, their places in time.

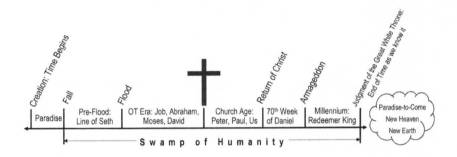

Markers that express periods of time will appear in this narrative and timeline, like the Flood or the giving of the Law. My point, however, is not about those markers in time but is about how those markers framed the lives of the men and women who occupied their part of time for the cause of redemption.

The first of these groups of individuals that rise above "swampy fallenness" is known as the line of Seth. These were individuals of spiritual renown before the Flood, like Enoch and Noah. During these roughly one thousand years, we know virtually nothing about people being redeemed out of the world's newfound fallenness and darkness. However, I believe that, since God has never been willing that any should perish, we will meet pre-diluvian saints in Heaven who were outside of the line of Seth. It is true that, at the end of this preflood period, there were only eight righteous men and women for God to save in the ark, but God had His witnesses, heroes of the faith, for every period of time.

Job stands out during the next era of fallen humanity as a major hero of righteousness. We always think of Job's patience and endurance. But do not forget that the world around him knew him because of his walk with God, and thus they knew God because of him, and the Kingdom expanded in Job's generation.

In the same way, Abraham stood out as a hero of faith. The rulers of Egypt and the Philistines, plus the lords of developing nations in Canaan, all feared him because of his relationship with his God, who became known as—the God of Abraham, Isaac, and Jacob. This understanding of God lasted until the time of Moses, when God gave a new Name to refer to Himself as Yahweh (YHWH). Similarly, the greatest monarch on the earth at that time, Pharaoh, had to acknowledge that Joseph had the Spirit of God in him, as God elevated Joseph to be one of the most influential persons in the world of his time (Genesis 41:38). Joseph's faithfulness to God gave God a platform for the entire world to see that He and He alone held the future in His hands. Many have wondered how a picture of God's greatness in that era of time would result in redeeming belief. I do not know the answer to that, but I am sure that it did result in belief, since God seeks people for eternal life (and always has) and has elevated His faithful ones while spreading His kingdom. These patriarchal heroes of the faith, and others like them, pointed their generations to the one true God who could redeem them from the slime of sin in humanity's swamp.

Moses, Gideon, Debra, Hannah, Samuel, David, Jehoshaphat, Hezekiah, and Josiah, along with prophets of the stature of Elijah, Elisha, Isaiah, and many others, were clear heroes of faith of their place in time. This faith was spelled out by the worship of Jehovah in His Law, and tabernacle, and temple, and by Israel, God's people themselves. Their story was often not pretty, but sin and the consequences of sin and a Redeemer for the people of the swamp became quite clear in the biblical narrative. Their stories are the era relating to the people who are of the lineage of the Christ, the Redeemer who was to come. This narrative reported how the children of the promise to Abraham would crawl out of the swamp, only to fall back in again. Then a hero of the faith would rise up as a leader or king or prophet and lead them on to the solidness of God's promises, only for the people to forget and slide back, often deeper in the muck of sin than they were before. This ongoing picture of God's grace and humanity's swampiness continued until Israel rejected and finally killed their Messiah, the One who came to save them. Little did Israel, or any living creature in the universe, know that this predicted slaughter of the Messiah, the Holy One, would become that timeless act of redemption. It was redemption for swamp dwellers past, present, and future if and when they surrendered to what God had revealed to *their* generation through the heroes of the kingdom of God.

This brings us to the Cross, and the death and burial and resurrection of the Redeemer, and the outpouring of the Redeemer's Spirit on His Church. These are, we are, the new people of God's own choosing (1 Peter 2:9). This era is known as the Church Age, and heroes of the faith like Peter, Paul, Priscilla and Aquila, James, Timothy, and Luke, the beloved physician, are characters of note in the book of Acts. As we all know, however, unlike any other book in the Bible, the book of Acts has no ending. That is because the story of the Church goes on with new heroes of the faith. These are men and women who may never be written about but are just as significant as Enoch, Debra, Jeremiah, Esther, Mary, Joseph, Peter, Paul, and other heroes of earlier eras of God's dealing with mankind. Men and women who were then, and men and women now, are just people like you and like me. We are the people God has chosen to do His mighty works in our part of our age, the Church Age.

Please get this point, or you have missed the message of this book. Earlier heroes and heroines of the faith were God's hands and feet and mouthpieces, spreading the Kingdom while they lived. Now, we are the hands and feet and mouthpieces of God designed to spread the Kingdom while we live. In His eternal plan, God has chosen to use humans as the vehicle for disseminating His Holy Word and His intentions. The history of the faith was His-story. Your faith-walk now, and my faith-walk now, are still His-story. In eternity, your life and my life will be parts of His-story of time. We are designed to be heroes of the faith. Jesus implied that when we lead someone out of the kingdom of darkness into the Kingdom of light, we are doing greater miracles than He did (John 14:12). It is clearly not important that a hero of our generation must have an official office or title, or be mentioned in the Bible, or have an honorable mention in the Church Age.

Hannah was just a young wife who became Samuel's mother and did not know her faith would be pivotal in Israel's history and in His-story, but it was. Esther was just an adopted teenaged girl forced into a bad situation that saved Israel, the nation of the seed of the Messiah. David was just a teenage boy taking cheese and bread to his brothers who were in the war, when he made history and became Israel's great king, the antecedent of the Christ. Andrew, Peter, James, and John were just doing their job as fishermen when the Great Rabbi called them to be fishers of men, resulting in their becoming heroes of the Church Age. What are you "just doing" as the Spirit of God is calling you to be a hero of the faith for your part in the Church Age? Our daily faithfulness in serving God and connecting dots for the souls of the people around us may not seem to be much now, but it is the way that heroes of the faith live, and the way Christ's Spirit spreads the gospel. The above is a little piece of history or His-story to date. Now, let's talk now about some geography of God spreading the message of the gospel.

The early Church record just after the day of Pentecost gives us a little pattern of how God will work to keep the Message expanding and expanding. The book of Acts begins with Jesus telling the eleven apostles, on behalf of all the church to come, that they were to be His witnesses in Jerusalem, Judea, Samaria, and to the ends of the earth. In Church Age dogma, we know well these words to be a geography lesson of the spreading and the growth of the gospel. It has been properly personalized to mean our immediate home turf, expanding ever farther out to encompass some level of accountability for the entire world to hear the Good News. Every person cannot go everywhere, but in the big picture, we need to be aware of the needs of the spread of the gospel elsewhere in the world and to participate in meeting those needs wherever we can. The letters of Paul and the book of Acts give plenty of object lessons of this participation by the sharing of resources and manpower between churches from country to country. If, however, the mandate to the early Church can be transposed and applied accurately to our lives as modern-day Christians, then we need to know that the same kind of application applies to the painful prodding the Spirit of Jesus had to do to get the early Church to move out. Let me explain.

Acts 1:8 carries that command from Jesus about going, and where to go, just before he ascended into Heaven. There is no apparent movement out of Jerusalem, however, until chapter 8, after the account of the murder of Stephen, which begins partway through chapter 6. I have not researched this myself, but some Bible scholars say that chapter 8 occurs twelve years after Christ's ascension and the command to spread the gospel. At that point, we see Saul, who later was renamed Paul, introduced at the stoning of Stephen. As Saul, we see God using him for His purpose even though he was the gospel's major opponent at that point in his life. Saul and others seriously escalate violence and persecution against the early Church. This began forcing the Church's people to move out of Jerusalem and spread the gospel elsewhere (Acts 8:1-4 and 11:19). It took severe trouble from Saul and others in Jerusalem, with death and imprisonments, to get the Church to obey the next step of Jesus' commandment to go and be witnesses in the rest of the world. It is interesting to me that when Saul became the apostle Paul, he experienced the very thing that he had been forcing on the Church earlier in his life. Throughout history, persecution has been a motivator and purifier for the Church to obey their Master.

Should we be surprised, then, when God does something similar in the lives of individual Christians like you and me? Jesus said to His disciples in Matthew 10 that they should be wise as serpents but harmless as doves because men were going to try to do them harm. The apostle Paul, in 2 Timothy 3:12, tells us that godliness will bring persecution, and in 2 Corinthians 12, Paul speaks of God's work in his own life because of a "thorn in the flesh" allowed by God to keep his heart in the right place. Today, many Christian leaders tell of heartbreaking circumstances that God allowed in their lives to get them to the place where God could use them or move them. As a soul winner, am I saying that you must suffer greatly? No, I don't think so. But do not be shocked if God nudges you because you have been stuck too long in one thing or another, and He wants you to move out. Anything that God allows or brings into our lives can seem tough for a while, but it will ultimately be for the cause of the spread of the Kingdom, and most often leaves us in a much better spot than we were before. We can ask for the tough stuff to end, that is our right as a child of God, but if God says no, then we must put on our big boy pants and march on. The kingdom of the King of Love must be served, so march on.

My personal story on this subject took place when I was thirty-six years old. I had been legally blind since childhood but completely functional in ministry, having planted my first church when I was 17 years old while still in Africa. After college, Carol and I were married and immediately went into church ministry. We had already planted one church together, and assisted in two others, and worked on staff in a church in California for four and a half years. We were well into another very exciting church plant when I discovered, through two painful accidents while I was running, that I was losing the rest of my sight and would be completely blind within ten years.

My church family wanted to pray for my healing and anoint me with oil, a practice described in James 5. I agreed to their idea because I also believed in and taught on this biblical practice. The following Sunday night, the elders, while surrounded by my wife and several dozen of the church family, anointed me and prayed for me to be healed. We had, together as a church, seen several instances of the wonderful power of God in healing during our time in that church. There was also a time or two in this process when God said no to our request for healing. As the elders and church family gathered around me to anoint me with oil and ask God for my healing from going blind, we were all aware that God could say yes or no. As His children, we ask the Father, but it is His final decision whether healing is His will or not.

The Sunday night when the anointing and prayer took place, I was so very optimistic. We all went home with expectations. The next morning, I awakened with a pleasant sensation that all was well. Before I opened my eyes, I rolled up onto my elbow, facing Carol. I wanted the first thing that I would see clearly to be my beloved wife of fifteen years. When my eyes were fully open, I realized that she was just as blurry as the day before. I did not know how to feel at that moment. I got up and walked around the end of the bed toward the door, then heard a voice. It said out loud, "I can use you better blind than with sight." That is all it said. I stopped and listened for more words, and Carol stirred because her sleep had been partially interrupted by the voice. Baffled, I continued to walk toward the door because I realized the voice I had heard, although clearly from God, had come out of my own mouth, using my own voice box. I knew for sure then that all was well, just not the well that we had asked for.

Sure enough, as the doctors predicted, I became entirely blind within ten years. But right after I heard the voice saying God could use me better blind, I felt certain that He could not possibly want me to keep planting churches while completely blind. So, while continuing on in that church ministry, I spent months asking the Lord for His next assignment. I prayed and searched my heart and asked and asked again for His new plan for my life. One morning, while on my knees and before the household awakened, I got my answer in silence. No words, but just as clear. The silence was my answer. I was to continue doing my part of spreading and growing the Kingdom right here in this church until He nudged me on, which He did a few years later. God wanted me to continue planting churches even while totally blind. After all, He had not changed my gifting or my call, and He had given me the best helpmeet (wife) possible for this clear assignment. So, in those following years, I retooled by learning Braille and other technologies for the blind. I soldiered on and am still doing so. Even without sight, I must admit, this is a much better way for me. I do not know what I would have been like if I had been healed that Sunday night, but God knows, and He said, "I can use you better blind than with sight." So be it.

God's kingdom will spread and grow and continue until God declares this age to be done. In the meantime, God will continue to use weak, fallen, rough, ordinary people like us to do extraordinary things for the spread and growth of His kingdom. If we want to be a part of His ever-expanding kingdom, we must let go of our pathetic attempts to run our own lives, and we must completely trust His directing of our lives. Then, and then only, will we become the heroes and heroines of faith for our generation. If God nudges, we must move. If He gives, we must graciously receive. If He takes away, we need to say, "Thy will be done." If He says to go, we need to say, "Point the way." God's sovereign plan is infinitely better than ours, and it will relate to His kingdom.

After all is said and done, as we someday look back on our

little piece of history, we will notice everything going on in the world was about His Story of redemption, which includes *all* the circumstances of our lives. A man sowed a mustard seed into his field. A woman put leaven into three measures of flour. God spreads, grows, and expands His own kingdom, but He has regular and ordinary people start the process.

CHAPTER 11
PATHWAYS TO CHRIST'S WAY

Many years ago, I was in Portland, Oregon, attending a conference at a hotel near the airport. I was scheduled to say a few words during the evening session, but I had been so engaged with coworkers that I had not prepared my thoughts and comments. The leaders wanted me to speak and inspire the crowd about church planting in seven minutes or less. My friend who had come with me convinced me that I could work on my thoughts while he drove us around in search of a place to eat. He headed south on 82nd Avenue while I quietly prayed for God to give me insight into what He wanted to say through me. By God's grace, the concept unfolded in front of me.

It was dusk and drizzly, and we found ourselves slowing down behind a sea of red brake lights. A detour sign forced everyone into the right lane to turn into a neighborhood. We followed suit. After one block, the line of detoured cars turned left to go parallel with 82nd. We obediently did the same thing. A few hundred feet down the road, we found ourselves following the line of brake lights leading us into a large cul-de-sac. Making a large counterclockwise loop, we headed back out from where we had just been. Like everyone else, when we got back to the original detour street, we waited our turn to go left and cut through the line of detouring cars to keep going the way we should have gone in the beginning. I asked my friend if he thought we should indicate to the stream of cars turning into the cul-de-sac that where they were going was a dead-end. He smiled at me and said, "Nah." Right then, I knew this was to be the point of my talk. God wanted me to tell my observations about how churches so often are misled because they are following other churches' ideas rather than seeking the Lord's face about what He wanted them to do in their *own* communities. I have seen churches follow the brake lights of other churches into one dead-end outreach idea after another, with little to no benefit. They followed human-made programs from other churches rather than trusting God to lead them into His plan for them. A great theologian said that churches have a fascination with sameness.

Maybe you have heard this illustration before, but it bears repeating. When tuning different types of pianos from a tuning fork, if the first piano is tuned to the fork, and then the second piano is tuned from the first piano, and the third piano is tuned from that second piano, and so on, you will find that when all the pianos are played together, the result is not perfect unison but something more like discord. However, if each piano is tuned individually to the tuning fork itself, there will be the perfection of sound, not discord. The apostle John, in his Gospel, says in 14:26, "But the Helper, the Holy Spirit, whom the Father will send in My name, He will teach you all things, and bring to your remembrance all that I have said to you" (NKJV).

Paul, in Acts 16:7, identifies that Spirit as being the actual Spirit of Jesus. Now, if the Spirit of Jesus is the Church's "tuning fork," then that church's ministry and outreach will ring true and be in tune with what Christ wants for that local church—not some other church's ministry. As churches, we must let our lead come from Jesus' Spirit, tuning us up for who we are, rather than becoming tuned to another "piano" no matter how impressive that piano might be.

In this chapter, I am going to show you the gospel principles taken from the life of Jesus that have governed our practice as a couple in planting churches over forty-plus years. These types of principles have worked in every place we have served throughout all those years. I will include a sample of how each principle taken from Jesus' ministry was interpreted and applied by us or others that I am talking about. Because I am blind and do not drive, following taillights is not something I have personally done. But I can tell you that in real life, I have tried not to follow the "taillights" of other ministries in the churches God called us to. We have wanted to be "in tune" with what I believed to be the model contained in the concept of being Christ's now-body in our world. Clearly, in being Christ's body, we must follow His high values. It is also clear that as individuals and churches, we cannot imitate the exact same actions that Jesus did while He was in His body. Still, the reasons and motivations behind His actions give us the direction that we can apply to our individual circumstances.

In Acts 13:36, Paul, in a sermon in Antioch in Pisidia, said that king David had "...served the purpose of God in his own generation...." According to my concordance, the word "purpose" can also be translated as "counsels" or "motivations." I am saying here that we must learn from the writings of the Gospels what Christ's purposes, counsels, and motivations were in doing what He did. By discovering what these motivations in the Gospels are, we can apply them to the ministry circumstances that we find in front of us, either as individuals or as churches. I feel strongly that I need to know the work of Jesus while He was here on earth, which means, no matter what book of the Bible I may be studying at any given time, I will also include reading the Gospels so as to know Him. All His motivations, counsels, and purposes are there as examples for His Body. I am going to try to make this point by stating the principle and giving a true personal example to go with it.

This first principle is found in the story of Jesus' encounter with a leper. This story is found in three out of the four Gospels. We will look at the one in Mark 1:40-42. Not only did Jesus hear the request of the leper and heal him, but Jesus *touched* him, too. This act modeled by Jesus was never done in society, and it was a touch the man had probably not experienced since he was diagnosed with leprosy. Following Christ's example, churches and individuals have asked themselves, "Who is an example of this man in our community? Who is the undesirable and outcast person who needs our touch?" I know of suburban churches that have identified *this man* for themselves as the homeless community that was not at their own doorstep but a few miles away in downtown. These churches would then do an occasional outreach gesture by making up gift packages of food and clothing and take them to the city and hand them out to the homeless. Certainly, this is one way of reaching out, but usually, it ends up being a bridge to nowhere. I say this because there is no follow-up. In actuality, this cost the church almost nothing, except some time and energy and maybe a little bit of finances. Such an outreach is between that church and God and is not to be judged by me. But the point I am making is this. As a church, we usually do not have to go miles away to find a symbolic leper. They are usually right in our own immediate world as a church.

Rob was *that man* for Carol and me. He was homeless, so Carol and I took him into our home. We still had small children, and we would not have taken this chance if it weren't for the other, more stable young men in our home at the time, who acted as a shield for the household. Rob was a dark character. He doodled every time he sat down for a few minutes. Using black ink, he would doodle evil pictures of devils and monsters and hellfire. He was with us less than a month, but we were not sure that we had helped him as much as we would have wanted to. Before he left our home, Rob did make a profession of faith. However, several years later, we learned he ended his own life in a forest using a gun. Though this was sad news, Carol and I knew that when we first met Rob that God wanted us to reach out and touch this man. It is my hope that Rob's profession of faith was a real indication that he actually trusted in Christ for salvation and that we will see him in Heaven someday. I look forward to finding out for sure.

Another easily transferable principle is found in Luke 23:39-43, where the Bible tells the account of three crosses. One bore the Savior. Another, a scoffer. And the third, a sinner saved by grace, who, while actively dying, turns to Jesus and surrenders his soul by saying, "Jesus, remember me when you come into your kingdom." And Jesus receives his surrender and promises him paradise. The principal question again is this, "Who might this person be in our immediate world?" Who do you know is physically, actively dying?

For me, the actively dying soul was Jeff. His wife Myrtle had received Christ and was struggling to set her drinking problem behind her, but she was truly saved and was growing in Christ. Jeff, on the other hand, was a good ol' boy and had been a reasonably successful businessman. In fact, in his mind, he felt he was better than his wife. I had several very amicable meetings with him during which we discussed the gospel, but each time ended in him strongly denouncing his need for Christ. After about a year of these conversations, he was diagnosed with stage four lung cancer. One of the last times I ever met with him face-to-face, I remember a statement he made to me very well. He said, "Harry, I know that I'm a sinner, and I know that I'm trying not to die. I'm pretty sure what you're telling me about getting to Heaven is true, but I've never asked anyone for help before, and I am not going to start now."

Shortly after this last face-to-face conversation with Jeff, his wife took him to a cancer clinic in Mexico that boasted a miraculous therapy, which was not available in the US. There are, of course, people who criticize or put down a death bed salvation, but I am not one of them. The thief on the cross gives me the understanding from the Bible that God does not either. Churches and individuals have taken this principle of the thief on the cross as their reason for choosing to minister in the area of hospice or hospital visitation. Why not? This is biblically indicated behavior for Christ's now-body, by imitating those actions when He was in His own physical body, and in this instance, his ministering to the dying thief on the cross.

Jeff had not been at the special cancer clinic in Mexico very long when I got a tearful call from his wife where she told me that he had taken a sudden turn for the worse. The doctor explained to her that Jeff would not last through the night, and she should come and sit with him so that he would not die alone. I asked Myrtle if she would mind if I prayed with her that God would give Jeff one more chance. She agreed, so I prayed with Myrtle out loud on the phone that evening, asking God to give Jeff one more opportunity to surrender to Him. The following morning at about 5 a.m., Pacific Time, my phone rang. It was Myrtle. She said, "You are not going to believe what's happened! An hour ago, Jeff came out of his coma and sat up. He asked for something to drink. The doctors are surprised, because nothing's really changed other than he woke up and has energy to sit up and talk." I reminded her of our prayer the night before, and she assured me she was fully aware of what God was doing. At this point, you might have guessed; I asked Myrtle to give Jeff the phone, which she did. I asked Jeff if he was ready yet to surrender his pride and accept God's salvation. He eagerly agreed, and we prayed together as he repeated the words which he now believed. His weak raspy voice was speaking, and his heart was surrendering to Christ. Fifteen minutes after I got off the phone with Jeff, he was in Heaven. He was meeting Jesus, his new best friend who took him from death into eternal life. We should never doubt a clear salvation principle, as seen in the Gospels.

Here is an idea for your church. A great small group study would be to examine the Gospels for the specific purpose of looking at Christ's actions. In doing this, you will be learning ministry principles. After the group has cataloged them all, then look at your church's own community closely to see just how these ministry principles might be applied in your church. Not everything you come up with will be able to be done by your church immediately, but the best ideas will line up with the people and resources you already have in the church. When God sees your loving obedience of faith, just as you are, He will bring to your church the additional workers to meet the needs. Trust me on this. I have seen it happen. God will reward your faithfulness in smaller easier things, by giving you the resources and manpower to do the more complex.

A Roman centurion gives us insight into our next principle. From the text, we have no reason to believe this man had any kind of prior personal relationship with Jesus, but in Matthew 8:5-13, he calls on Jesus to perform an outrageous healing. He asked Jesus to say the word, and his servant, who was some distance away, would be healed. He did not ask for Jesus' touch on his servant or even His presence. He just asked Jesus to say the word, and his servant would be healed. That is exactly what Jesus did. Then Jesus told the people with him that the centurion had extraordinary faith, unlike any He had seen anywhere else in Israel.

While visiting homes in South Africa, my dad saw this kind of outrageous faith in a not-yet-believer. Let me tell you the story. Mrs. Denis was known in her immediate community as being a hard-driving, extremely loud, and vocal woman. She was flat on her back from cancer in her abdomen. She had exhausted what the medical profession in South Africa had to offer her at that time, so the doctors had sent her home to die. She and her husband had heard the name of an American man of God who was visiting in homes in their town, but they did not know how to reach him. That is, until one Sunday afternoon, there was a knock at their door. Mr. Denis answered the door. Seeing who it was, in his excitement, he neglected to say anything but left the door open while he ran back inside to his wife's room. My dad just stood there until he heard a female voice bellowing from a back bedroom. "Brother Olsen, please come in." Dad followed the voice and came in to see Mrs. Denis flat on her back in the bed and her husband standing on the other side of the bed with a sheepish grin on his face.

Without any explanation, Mrs. Denis said, "Give me your

hand!" She grabbed my dad's hand in hers and her husband's hand with her other hand. She put Dad's hand on her belly and said, "Brother Olsen, pray for my healing right here. The doctors sent me home to die." My dad, quite taken aback by her request, and now with his hand held tight in hers and touching her belly, boldly dove into a prayer for her healing. He did not at all understand what God was doing in that outrageous moment, but God did. A miracle took place.

As someone once said, "Now, the rest of the story." As it turned out, Mrs. Denis was the undisputed community matriarch and boss. When the word got out about her healing, almost every door in that entire neighborhood gladly opened when my dad knocked. Not only were Mr. and Mrs. Denis saved, many others were also. Bible studies opened up to Dad in a couple of places in the neighborhood.

This is not a unique situation because I know of some churches and other missionaries who give God the opportunity to show outrageous power in evangelism. They do things such as boldly going to a home and asking if they can pray for the household or anyone who may be sick in the home. Jesus, through accepting the outrageous faith-proposition of the centurion and displaying His miraculous power that day, has shown us, His now-body on earth, what His motivations and purposes continue to be. He wants us to see that He is willing to work great miracles to save souls He loves. Is there something of this magnitude that you or your church should consider since we have this principle in the Gospels?

In the Gospel of John, chapter 3, we see a totally different principle in the first twelve verses, using a different approach. A religious leader in Israel named Nicodemus comes quietly to Jesus by night with a theological question. Jesus does not blow him off but takes on his query headfirst. Some people suggest avoiding at all costs any theological debates that can turn into an argument, like this one with Nicodemus. They are quite right if one is trying to argue. In my experience, no one has ever been argued into the Kingdom. Still, in the past, I have actually created circumstances that follow the Nicodemus pattern because people with real questions are triggered by their past religious experiences. Their spiritual journey needs to be respected.

Once, in a small town in the Northwest, I took on this kind of theological, cultural, spiritual need. This is the way I approached it. I paid for a space in the local weekly newspaper so I could write a weekly article. The title I chose was "Issues with Answers." There were very interesting results from the articles I wrote on biblical answers to current cultural issues. My most interesting response was from a small monastery in the mountains where the Brothers were under a vow of silence but were allowed to write letters. One of them wrote to tell me that the high point of the week was when the paper came, and the Brothers took turns reading my article. He told me they loved that weekly "look outside of their cloister" and "a theological discussion of the contemporary issue."

However, the best response by far to my articles was when Kent, the editor of the paper, came to know Christ as his Savior. He was a man in his late thirties. Kent's journey toward salvation began with reading the articles with a critical eye. But over many months, he slowly began to surrender to the truth, which resulted in him attending our church. After a few weeks, Kent came to me after a service and wanted to be saved. He had accumulated many questions about the faith of his believing wife and found them mostly answered over time through the articles. There was no debate, no arguing, just truth to ponder.

After a year or so of weekly articles in this local paper, I found a way to speak with some of my readers. I found a venue in an enclosed section of the foyer of a historic hotel in town. I chose a date and then advertised the time we would start meeting weekly. The time together would be for open discussions on *The Bible Versus the Humanist Manifesto*. I was pleased with the responses to the topic, and over a period of time, these discussions about the Bible perspective led to conversations about the gospel. We must realize the Bible has the answers, but there are times when we need to let people work through their ignorance and then hold it up to the light of scripture, letting the words of Jesus, through His Spirit, do its own work. This approach to the need for theological discussion in that community did not come from some other church's taillights from somewhere else. It came from Jesus' example in John Chapter 3.

Are you getting the picture yet? We do not have to search contemporary Christian culture to find ideas to reach our world. God's purposes, councils, and motivations can be seen in the scriptures. Especially the Gospels. Examine His Word and apply His motivation to *your* specific and immediate community and its needs. Then, using the resources that God has already built into your body of believers, make your plan.

Another basic principle and motivation of Christ we see in the Gospels is that Jesus is the Light of the world (John 8:12). In another Gospel, Jesus says to His followers that *they* are the light of the world (Matthew 5:14-16). In verse 15, Jesus shows the true strength of His light inside His followers by indicating that it takes an outside obstruction to dull the strength of the light within them. He simply makes His point by commanding them not to cover the light with a basket. This concept is just as true for a body of believers as it is for an individual.

Let me introduce you to my friend Leonard. Even though I knew he would never feel he should be, I asked him if I could include him in this book. He humbly said yes. In my nearly three decades of knowing him, I can think of no one who better personifies being light than he does. Everywhere and in every way, I have seen him live life according to Jesus' command found in verse 16, which is the next verse of this passage (Matthew 5), "Let your light shine before others, so that they may see your good works and give glory to your Father who is in heaven."

Wherever Leonard is, at the front desk of his business, or in a restaurant, or on vacation in Mexico, or training recruits in his field of business, the radiance of Christ's presence in his life leads to spiritual conversations, which in many cases results in people desiring to know Christ as Savior. In his personal life, Leonard's kindness and generosity, and forthrightness have led many individuals to believe that God really loves them. I know beyond a shadow of a doubt there will be many people in Heaven because of the light of Christ they saw in him. And more than that, Leonard was able and always willing to share and explain how they too could have this light in them.

Being the light is such a fundamental principle in the Gospels, namely that each one of us can radiate the light of Christ in our own worlds. The scripture is clear. When we are not being light, it is not because Jesus' light in us has dimmed; it is because we have let an obstruction to the light build up. Christ's light seen in Christians is there to attract people to Him. The design is simple; every believer is equipped to be beautifully attractional people in their community by Christ's light shining through their person. In actuality, according to this same design, it takes a lot on our part to make the light in us be *less* than attractive. Many, many people's pathways to Christ have either begun or been completed by observing the radiance of Christ in the individuals of His now-body on Earth. The principle of this light is that we do not have to put on a show of brightness; we simply need to get the junk in our lives out of the way of Christ's light that is already there.

Now, this last principle I want to bring up is a difficult and very specific principle to understand. It is implied when Jesus, in both Matthew and Luke, tells His disciples to do something that is confusing to Western thinking. He tells them that, when doing ministry, they were not to make financial plans but to trust Him. Matthew 10:9 says, "Provide neither gold nor silver nor copper in your money belts" (NKJV). Luke 9:3 says, "...Take nothing for the journey, neither staffs nor bag nor bread nor money; and do not have two tunics apiece" (NKJV). Luke 10:4 says, "Carry neither money bag, knapsack, nor sandals..." (NKJV).

It might be difficult today to strictly operate as stated in these commands of Jesus to His 12 or His 72 disciples, respectively, as He sent them out. But there is a financial faith principle in these passages. We followed it in one of our church plants.

The church plant had acquired land. All of the essential approvals from the county had been met. Then, an opportunity came up for acquiring modular buildings from a school, which had used them for temporary classrooms. These classrooms would work well for the first phase of our church as educational space, that could also be used for our services to begin with. The price was quite reasonable, but the church plant had minimal cash reserves. We had enough to purchase the modules and move them to our lot, but that was it. I took the problem to the men I was training to become elders. They looked at the situation from every angle, but the site preparation and development would cost us $113,000.00—more than we had. After there has been a discussion, my practice in times like this is to table the topic for a week until our next scheduled meeting. I asked the elders to pray about it. In this context, praying about it was not hyperbole but a somber commitment.

There were no new ideas at the next meeting, just a sense that God was bigger than this need. When the elders and I got up off our knees, having given the issue over to the Lord once again, I told the guys that a strange thought had come to me

during prayer. I told them what this thought was and suggested
we would pray again for another week before we readdressed
the issue. The thought I had was based on that strange principle in Matthew and Luke I quoted earlier—to trust Him
financially. What if we focused on people getting saved and left
the funding problem to the Lord? The principle from Christ's
ministry would be addressed in our situation like this. We
would use the money we had to purchase the modular units,
and to arrange for them to be transported a hundred miles to
our plot of ground. The financial shortfall we would handle in
the following manner:

Since we needed $113,000.00, we would go ahead as if we
already had it, and we would not look for money for our
problem but commit ourselves to work towards leading at least
113 people to Christ during the upcoming year. There would be
no loans, fundraisers, bonds issued, or anything else that
churches typically do to raise capital funds. There would just be
prayer and evangelistic outreach. We would focus on prayer and
the principles in the above passages to work on people being
saved, and leave the financial issue to the Lord, based on the
implications of what Jesus said to His followers about not
making their plans around money but around serving Him. It
was a special moment. There was no discord, only a calm and
spine-tingling sense that maybe God wanted to do something
extraordinary.

A week later, we met again to make a decision. Once again,
we rose from our knees and committed to this act of faith,
knowing that this was going to be our faith-building adventure.

For the sake of time, let me summarize by saying that a year later, the church's first building was in place and occupied and paid for in full. The string of miraculous events that had funded the finishing of the church is a story in and of itself. But the best part was that the church was almost already full because of the 115 professions of faith during that year! The salvation stories, of course, are even more exciting; God's grace repeated over and over again.

In this chapter, I have bombarded you with all these great accounts of God's work to make one overarching point. The best ministries that lead to salvations are modeled after and follow from the Gospels as principles of ministry demonstrated in Jesus when He was in His ministry years and in His earthly body. A church or an individual does not need to slavishly follow what other churches or soul winners have done. They need to let God personalize, through His Spirit, the approach to getting His work of evangelism done. His purposes, counsels, and motivations are clear. Remember, following taillights could well have a person or a church finding themselves going down a dead-end.

Let me wrap up this book by saying, the mindset of a soul winner begins and ends with the fact that saving souls is God's work and we are just participants in the story of redemption. Jesus said that we are to seek first His kingdom and if we do, the stuff of life around us will fall under His kind administration. His life story of redemption He has passed on to us, His now-body, and we are to live that story out intentionally and with expectations. There are *empty seats* in our lives that He wants to fill with individuals that He is preparing for salvation. God is not asking us to save those people, but to connect the dots of the picture of Jesus and His salvation, just the dots that He puts in front of us. And *He* will save them at the right time. He has given us incredible tools to work with for our part in all of this, culminating in prayer, which is our daily act of faith.

The Spirit of Jesus Christ is preparing more souls for eternal life than there are laborers willing to invite those souls to surrender to His atoning work on the Cross. Let's step it up a notch and give God a chance to make us spiritual heroes in our generation by accomplishing His purpose of seeking for salvation all who are lost.

ACKNOWLEDGMENTS

This book could not have happened without my daughter, Rebekah Lind, and her hard work and dedication to this book project on every level.

My wife Carol worked on making the book a kinder, gentler record of ministry events in which, much of the time, she was a participant with me.

My grandson Kaleb did the original drawing inside the book. Other work by him can be seen on Instagram @artbykalebl.

Finally, three faithful friends, Rod Shockley, Deblyn Freemon, and Dr. Joel Bundick, all with ministry and theological standing, read my manuscript and gave input in the areas of theological and biblical accuracy, as well as usability in ministry.

I thank all of you very much.

ABOUT THE AUTHOR

Harry Olsen was raised as a missionary kid in Africa. He actively served alongside his parents and siblings in the ministry. After his theological training at Multnomah Bible College in Portland, Oregon, and where he met his wife, Carol, who also attended Multnomah, they went immediately into full time church planting.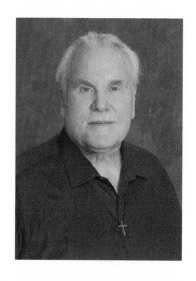

Together they planted seven churches with at least five more church starts spinning off of the churches they started. Harry's experience in starting churches led to formal oversight of church planting, stationing them in Denver, Colorado, for many years.

Harry's foremost concern about ministry these days is the lack of intentional soul winning and biblical ignorance in many churches, so in 2013, he founded a training college targeting men and women in their 30's, 40's or and 50's who desire to be in church planting, pastoral ministries, or just to serve the Lord better as leaders in their churches.

This hybrid live and online training program focuses on Bible, theology, and ministry preparation. The training program was created with a clear focus on church planting and evangelism, but Harry found that Christian leaders in their churches responded with enthusiasm because church planter training could enhance *all* ministry efforts. You can visit the website at www.cbmatrix.org.

Made in the USA
Middletown, DE
10 September 2021